THE INTERVAL

The Interval

RELATION AND BECOMING IN IRIGARAY, ARISTOTLE, AND BERGSON

Rebecca Hill

Fordham University Press
NEW YORK ‡ 2012

Library of Congress Cataloging-in-Publication Data

Hill, Rebecca.
The interval : relation and becoming in Irigaray, Aristotle, and Bergson / Rebecca Hill. — 1st ed.
p. cm.
Includes bibliographical references (p.) and index.
ISBN 978-0-8232-3724-1 (cloth : alk. paper)
1. Irigaray, Luce. 2. Sex differences 3. Irigaray, Luce. Ethique de la différence sexuelle. 4. Aristotle. 5. Bergson, Henri, 1859–1941. I. Title.
B2430.I74.H55 2012
176—dc22

2011016592

Printed in the United States of America
14 13 12 5 4 3 2 1
First edition

CONTENTS

ABBREVIATIONS

Irigaray

English Texts

ESD *An Ethics of Sexual Difference*. Translated by Carolyn Burke and Gillian C. Gill (1993)

ILTY *I Love to You: Sketch of a Possible Felicity in History*. Translated by Alison Martin (1996)

IR *The Irigaray Reader*. Edited by Margaret Whitford (1991)

JTN *Je, Tu, Nous: Toward a Culture of Difference*. Translated by Alison Martin (1993)

S *Speculum of the Other Woman*. Translated by Gillian C. Gill (1985)

TS *This Sex Which Is Not One*. Translated by Catherine Porter with Carolyn Burke (1985)

WL *The Way of Love*. Translated by Heidi Bostic and Stephen Pluháček (2002)

French Texts

CS *Ce sexe qui n'en est pas un* (1977)

E *Éthique de la différence sexuelle* (1984)

SA *Speculum de l'autre femme* (1974)

Bergson

English Texts

CE *Creative Evolution*. Translated by Arthur Mitchell (1983)

CM *The Creative Mind: An Introduction to Metaphysics*. Translated by Mabelle L. Andison (1992)

ME *Mind-Energy*. Translated by H. Wildon Carr (1920)

MM *Matter and Memory*. Translated by Nancy Margaret Paul and W. Scott Palmer (1981)

TFW *Time and Free Will: An Essay on the Immediate Data of Consciousness*. Translated by F. L. Pogson (1913)

French Texts

O *Œuvres* (1959)

M *Mélanges*. Edited by André Robinet (1972)

Other Authors

B Deleuze. *Bergsonism*. Translated by Hugh Tomlinson and Barbara Habberjam (1991)

BE Deleuze. *Le Bergsonisme* (1968)

BI Olkowski. "The End of Phenomenology: Bergson's Interval in Irigaray" (2000)

BP Mullarkey. *Bergson and Philosophy* (1999)

GL Ansell-Pearson. *Germinal Life: The Difference and Repetition of Deleuze* (1999)

FSD Butler, Cornell, Cheah, and Grosz. "The Future of Sexual Difference: An Interview with Judith Butler and Drucilla Cornell" (1998)

ID Deutscher. *A Politics of Impossible Difference: The Later Work of Luce Irigaray* (2002)

MP Derrida. *Margins of Philosophy*. Translated by Alan Bass (1982)

NB Mullarkey, ed. *The New Bergson* (1999)

NT Grosz. *The Nick of Time: Politics, Evolution, and the Untimely* (2004)

TT Grosz. *Time Travels: Feminism, Nature, Power* (2005)

OBT Cheah and Grosz. "Of Being-Two" (1998)

RR Olkowski. The Ruin of Representation (1999)

ACKNOWLEDGMENTS

I am grateful to Helen Tartar for her interest and belief in this project. My colleagues and students in the School of Media and Communication at RMIT University deserve thanks for providing a supportive and stimulating environment in which to work. I am indebted to Ewa Plonowska Ziarek and Alison Ross for reading and commenting on earlier drafts of the whole manuscript. Thanks to Claire Colebrook, Linda Daley, and Kristin Sampson for conversations that helped me to shape my thinking in this book. I wish to acknowledge Liz Grosz for her friendship and encouragement during the long gestation of this project. Her comments on various drafts of the manuscript and the inspiration of her scholarship and teaching have been invaluable to the evolution of my thinking on the interval. Megan Eastlake, Imogen Williams, Dianne Currier, Kate McDonald, Kelly Pearson, Jami Weinstein and Belinda Smaill have my gratitude for their hospitality and friendship. Thanks also to my parents Christina and John Hill and my sister Melissa Hill. I particularly wish to thank Elizabeth Lamb for her love, generosity, and companionship.

An earlier version of Chapter Five, "Interval, Sexual Difference" appeared as "Interval, Sexual Difference" in *Hypatia: A Journal of Feminist Philosophy* 23, no. 1 (Winter 2008). An earlier version of Chapter Six, "Phallocentrism in Bergson," appeared as "Phallocentrism in Bergson" in "Deleuze and Gender," ed. Claire Colebrook and Jami Weinstein, special issue, *Deleuze Studies* 2, supplement (2008).

THE INTERVAL

Introduction

THE CONCEPT OF THE "INTERVAL" in English and in French (*l'intervalle*) has both spatial and temporal senses, which are by no means discrete. Frequently, the interval designates a mere gap. An interval is a break between two events or actions in time, or, in extensive terms, an interval is an empty space between two things.[1] Whether construed as spatial or temporal, the interval is presumed to be calculable and homogeneous. The conceptualization of the interval as a calculable gap in time or in space is precisely what I will be arguing against in these pages. Instead, I suggest a heterogeneous figuration of the interval overflowing all attempts at presentation. This book argues for a formulation of the interval as the generative threshold of space and time, as the very motor of difference preceding any designation of identity, and as the place of the possibility of sexual difference.

My interest in the interval emerged in response to reading Luce Irigaray's *An Ethics of Sexual Difference*. In this groundbreaking text, she situates the task of articulating the question of sexual difference—which is *the* question of her oeuvre, the question that would, perhaps, enable the emergence of a new age of thought and life—in terms of a radical rethinking of the interval. She writes:

> The transition to a new age requires a mutation in the perception and conception of *space-time*, our inhabitation of *places*, and the different *envelopes of identity*. It assumes and entails an evolution or transformation of forms, of the matter-form relationship and of the interval *between* (them): the trilogy of our constitution of place. Each age assigns limits to this trinity, be they *matter*, *form*, *interval* or *power* (*puissance*), *act*, interval-intermediate. (Translation modified; IR, 167/E, 15)

Thinking through the implications of this aphoristic passage is the primary task of this book. This is a difficult undertaking because the interval cannot be assigned a permanent definition. For Irigaray, the interval needs to be conceived as the very attractions, tensions, and acts between form and matter and also as the remainder (*reste*) that subsists after each oeuvre and *between* what is already identified and what remains to be identified (IR, 167–68/E, 15–16). In this respect, any attempt at a definition of the interval would amount to suppressing the interval's specific dynamics.

To my knowledge there is no major study devoted to thinking through the implications of Irigaray's call to reconceive the interval in *Ethics*.[2] Perhaps this is why she is often characterized as a thinker of subjectivity concerned above all else with the question of "who speaks?"[3] Her critique of metaphysics as phallocentrism does argue that every theory of the subject has been appropriated by the masculine (S, 133–46/SA, 165–82). But Irigaray's critical description proceeds less from pointing out "who speaks" and more from a careful consideration of the interval or relationship between the metaphysical tradition and the condition that she argues philosophy has repressed. According to her well-known position, Western metaphysics has posited a conceptual edifice that is isomorphically congruent with a phallocentric male body, while everything in the tradition recalling the female sex is denigrated. Obliquely, the phallic architecture of philosophy is dependent on the disavowal of the maternal-feminine.[4] Irigaray's critical description of metaphysics is concerned with thinking through this relationship or interval, which secretly designates the maternal-feminine as the ground on which philosophy is erected as phallocentrism. One of my aims is to trace the evolution of her engagement in this task in her early critical work in *Speculum* to *Ethics*, where the interval is figured as the very opening to the possibility of sexual difference.

Irigaray's call to think the interval in *Ethics* can be read beyond her critique of the subject as phallocentric and beyond her theorization of sexed intersubjectivity. Irigaray thinks the interval as an open threshold. The interval can be conceived as a place of the possibility of subjectivity and intersubjectivity, the interval can also be conceived as a threshold of the becoming of sexed forces. Further, a close reading of Irigaray suggests the interval and sexual difference are not substitutable.

In other words, Irigaray's formulation of the interval is a thinking of difference that is not reducible to a theory of subjectivity. It is true, of course, that her work elaborates an intersubjective figuration of difference, especially in works published after the early eighties. She takes up the interval as the threshold for a nonhierarchical ethics of relations between woman and man. But even in her more recent writing, Irigaray emphasizes the openness of the interval beyond the figuration of subjectivity. For instance, in *The Way of Love*, she writes that sexual difference is "perhaps the most unthinkable of differences—difference itself" (WL, 106). While this phrase privileges sexual difference, her inscription of "perhaps" is crucial because it stops sexual difference from colonizing difference itself. "Perhaps" leaves the potential of the interval *open* within the terms of her argument. To acknowledge the open potential of the interval is to acknowledge that the interval can be conceived as a threshold for the theorization of different relations of alterity and different becomings by no means secondary to sexual difference.

This book focuses on the way in which Irigaray's interval can be read both as an opening to a nonhierarchical relation between woman and man and as the differentiating force of sexed becoming in excess of a theory of intersubjectivity. Irigaray does not explicitly develop an account of sexed becoming that is distinguished from sexed intersubjectivity. This task has been taken up by Elizabeth Grosz in essays such as "The Force of Sexual Difference" and "Inhuman Forces" from her book *Time Travels* (2005). Beyond the specific context of scholarship on Irigaray and the philosophy of sexual difference, I hope this book offers some fruitful insights for feminist theory on the question of how to think difference rigorously.[5]

While Irigaray's formulation of the interval orients the structure of the argument, this project is only partly devoted to a study of her corpus. Instead, I read Irigaray's thinking on the interval in relation to two male philosophers, Aristotle and Henri Bergson. Aristotle and Bergson are by no means feminist thinkers. Aristotle's metaphysics is infamously riven with phallocentric violence, and, though Bergson does not share his Greek predecessor's open contempt for women, I argue that his philosophy is also phallocentric. Despite the phallocentrism underwriting their projects, I suggest that reading Aristotle and

Bergson together with Irigaray is fruitful in the difficult task of conceptualizing the interval.

My decision to read Aristotle is motivated by the fact that he is the first philosopher to define the relationship between form (*morphē*) and matter (*hylē*), the interval (*diastēma*), and place (*topos*). Irigaray's contention that place is constituted by the matter–form relation and the interval between them draws directly on his presentation of these concepts (IR, 167/E, 15). Aristotle could be presented as the villain here because he explicitly designates the interval as secondary to the primacy of the identities of the categories of being. That is not how he is read in these pages. I argue that the status of the interval in Aristotle is highly ambiguous. On the one hand, his metaphysics suppresses the interval by presenting it as posterior to the identities of the categories. On the other hand, his discourse is marked by moments of oscillation in which the interval emerges, albeit fleetingly, in excess of its definition and beyond the being of any category. Drawing on Irigaray's "Place, Interval," I suggest his theory of *topos* can be radicalized and read to affirm the interval as a sensible relation and as the very condition of place, which is by no means secondary to the highest concepts of his ontology.

Irigaray does not engage with Bergson's philosophy specifically. Yet, as Dorothea Olkowski and Grosz have pointed out, there are significant affinities between Irigaray's and Bergson's respective projects (Olkowski BI; RR, 80–3; Grosz NT, 14). Bergson's thinking on the interval is, in some ways, remarkably resonant with Irigaray. Throughout his career, Bergson was preoccupied with theorizing time. Significantly for my purposes, he privileges a concept of the interval as the opening of time, or what he calls "duration" (*la durée*). For Bergson the interval of duration is nothing other than the threshold of intuition, the method he believes philosophy must pursue in order to become a rigorous form of knowledge. The Bergsonian interval is not subordinate to identity or calculability. On the contrary, his interval is the threshold of difference, space, and matter and exceeds all attempts at calculation and prediction.

Like Irigaray, Bergson ascribes fundamental importance to a formulation of the interval as the opening of thinking and life from which space and time might be reconceived. In contrast to Olkowski and

Grosz, I do not suggest that this striking resonance between them should be construed as a claim that Irigaray's conception of the interval is directly compatible with Bergson's interval and his method of intuition.[6] On the contrary, I argue that Bergson's contention that space and matter are products of the interval of duration is imbricated in phallocentric violence. For Irigaray, the interval is sexed and must be conceived as both spatial *and* temporal and material *and* transcendental.

This book is organized into two parts, "Relations" and "Becoming." The first part, "Relations," is devoted to Aristotle and to Irigaray's engagement with his oeuvre. In broad terms, it demonstrates that the interval of sexual difference is foundational to Aristotle's project and that this grounding "concept" must be thought as place or the possibility of place. Chapter One reads difference in Aristotle's metaphysics in relation to Irigaray's first essay on his work, "How to Conceive (of) a Girl?" (S, 160–7/SA, 200–9). Drawing on Irigaray, I argue that his explicit and well-known subordination of difference to identity is predicated on a phallocentric cover-up. The concepts he privileges—form, substance, identity, *physis*—are isomorphically congruent with phallic masculinity, while the concepts he designates as their subordinates—matter, privation, and difference—are entwined with a misogynist figuration of femininity. Yet the privilege of form, identity, and *physis* is far less secure than he admits. They stand on the repression of an interval, which covertly serves to distinguish Aristotle's phallic conceptual architecture from what Irigaray calls the maternal-feminine. I suggest Irigaray's critical description of this sexed hierarchy in "How to Conceive (of) a Girl?" unravels the hierarchical structure of his metaphysics without yet positing a way to conceive another thinking of difference that moves beyond phallocentrism.

The second chapter is a close reading of one of the most difficult texts in Aristotle's oeuvre, his treatise on place (*topos*), *Physics* 4.1–5. I argue that Aristotle, albeit briefly, and without apparently assimilating the implications of the maneuver, affirms that place—a sensible relation between two bodies that are different in being—is the ground of thinking. Aristotle insists this relation is not an interval (*diastēma*) but an immobile limit (*peras*) between two bodies. This is not, then, a thinking of the interval. Yet his affirmation of this relation as foundational is crucial—it underlines the inextricability of the sensible from a thinking of the interval, and it anticipates the grounding status of Irigaray's contention that place is an interval (*l'intervalle*).

Irigaray's "Place, Interval" is the focus of Chapter Three (ESD, 34–55/E, 41–59). This essay resumes the critical description of Aristotle that she began in "How to Conceive (of) a Girl?" Where her first essay stops short of proposing a way to figure a concept of difference as the threshold for a nonhierarchical sexuate relation, "Place, Interval" directly affirms the interval as the opening between woman and man, through which their relationship and their identities as sexed subjects are articulated. Irigaray's radicalization of Aristotle also posits a new conceptualisation of the matter–form relation. These formulations are developed through a radical rereading of Aristotle's argument in *Physics* 4.2–5. I suggest that, in some ways, Irigaray's interval is a tribute to Aristotle's legacy.

Part Two, "Becoming," is a reading of Bergson's philosophy of duration in relation to the question of sexual difference. Bergson explicitly elaborates duration through a rigorous formulation of the interval. While his figuration of the interval has some striking common resonances with Irigaray's interval of sexual difference, their approaches also diverge significantly. Chapter Four introduces his intuitive approach to metaphysics and his deduction of the interval of duration in his first major work, *Time and Free Will*. This chapter is particularly concerned with the dualism he establishes between consciousness and duration, on the one hand, and space and matter, on the other hand.

Chapter Five draws on Irigaray's critical description of metaphysics as phallocentrism to argue that Bergson's deduction of the duration of consciousness is predicated on a sexed hierarchy. Duration is posited in terms of paternal masculinity, and space (matter, the homogeneous) is denigrated and rendered as feminine in the phallocentric sense. And yet the privilege Bergson confers on duration is by means secure, because its elevation depends on the disavowal of heterogeneous spatiality or what I propose to call, after Irigaray, the maternal-feminine. The chapter concludes by rereading Bergson's deduction of the interval of duration as a sensible and transcendental difference that articulates a nonhierarchical relation between the sexes.

Bergson's philosophy is not reducible to a thinking of human consciousness. Chapter Six takes up his effort to go beyond the human condition in order to consider the extent to which phallocentrism continues to structure his project and to draw out of his thinking the aspects that might enable an escape from sexed hierarchy. My critique is not elaborated in order to shut Bergson down. On the contrary, I hope to reconceive his thinking of life and matter as a philosophy of material becoming.

The conclusion, "Interval as Relation, Interval as Becoming," traces the relationship between the concept of the interval as relation, addressed in Part One, and the concept of the interval as becoming, which is sketched in Part Two.

PART I

Relations

1. The Oblivion of the Interval

Whenever he [the Egyptian king, Sesostris] encountered a courageous enemy who fought valiantly for freedom, he erected pillars on the spot inscribed with his own name and country, and a sentence to indicate that by the might of his armed forces he had won the victory; if, however, a town fell easily into his hands without a struggle, he made an addition to the inscription on the pillar—for not only did he record on it the same facts as before, but added a picture of a woman's genitals, meaning to show that the people of that town were no braver than women.

HERODOTUS 1972, 104

The ethics of sexual difference are persistent and to come. In *all* patriarchal cultures, *all* classes. . . .

SPIVAK 1993, 191

To BEGIN A WORK ON THE INTERVAL—an interval that exceeds and precedes any designation of identity and would serve as the threshold of nonhierarchical sexual difference—with a close reading of Aristotle might be read as a pedestrian gesture. This would be the case if I presented him as a "straw man," the predictable villain for poststructuralist feminisms and thinkers of difference. After all, he is widely credited with formalizing dichotomous logic, and his work is infamously explicit about woman's servile relation to man (1254b13–4).[1] While I do not dispute these assessments of Aristotle, I do not begin with his philosophy merely to condemn him. On the contrary, following Irigaray's reading, I want to draw out a more interesting Aristotle. I want to consider what he has to offer to the theorization of the interval of sexual difference in excess of his misogyny.[2] Aristotle's metaphysics are understood here as an invaluable resource in the difficult task of articulating the place of the interval of sexual difference.

This chapter is concerned primarily with Aristotle's formalization of the relationship between identity and difference. I argue that his philosophy is highly ambivalent toward the interval. On the one hand, difference is subordinate to the identities of his cherished categories of being. On the other hand, there are moments in his discourse in which the interval is affirmed in excess of any designation of being.

His theorization of the relationship between identity (*to auto*) and difference (*diaphora*) is figured in sexuate terms. More precisely, his valorization of the identities of the concepts of substance (*ousia*), *physis*, and form (*eidos*, *morphē*) are presented as masculine, and his devaluation of matter (*hylē*) and privation (*sterēsis*)—their supposed opposites—are aligned with the feminine. As we will see, this sexed hierarchy is undermined by the moments in his discourse in which difference erupts beyond the constraints of the identities of the categories.

Toward the end of this chapter, I read the contradictory figuration of difference in Aristotle in relation to Irigaray's critical description of his metaphysics in her early work, "How to Conceive (of) a Girl?" (S, 160–67/SA, 200–09). In this essay, Irigaray shows how the "highest" concepts of his ontology—substance, *physis*, and form—are obliquely dependent on their devalued "opposites." I argue that "How to Conceive (of) a Girl?" is both a critique and a subversion of Aristotle. Irigaray makes explicit the phallocentrism enmeshed in his articulation of dichotomous logic *and* displaces the very functioning of that logic. Traces of the maternal-feminine overflow the limits of his ontology. This overflow, which cannot be presented as such, serves as the groundless ground of his project.

THE VIOLENCE OF BINARY LOGIC

As is well known, binary oppositions are logical contradictories symbolized by the relation of A and Not-A. The structure of this logic is formalized by Aristotle through the law of noncontradiction.

He writes that "the same attribute cannot at the same time belong and not belong to the same subject in the same respect" (1005a20). This means that one side of a contradictory (A) is always true while the other side (Not-A) is necessarily false. For example, the following statements are mutually exclusive: "he is sitting" and "he is not sitting" (11b23; 13b2).

Binary oppositions are characterized by the law of excluded middle, which prohibits the existence of a middle position between opposed propositions or terms. The excluded middle is the necessary empty space that separates A from Not-A (Jay 1981, 45). Its role is to keep A as a discrete identity uncontaminated by the infinitation of the negative characteristic of Not-A. As John Dewey writes, "If, say, 'virtue' be assigned to A as its meaning, then Not-A includes not only vice, but triangles, horseraces, symphonies and the procession of the equinoxes."[3] Here "Not-virtue" is denied specificity, except as the absence of A.

The excluded middle is supposed to maintain A as a discrete identity uncontaminated by the infinitation of the negative that defines Not-A. Yet, as critics of binary thought point out, A depends on Not-A to have meaning. A would have no identity as A without the designation of Not-A as its excluded other. In this sense, Not-A is not external to A but constitutive of its very identity. Thus, despite Aristotle's intentions, his cherished principle of excluded middle does not hold. I will analyze the implications of this unacknowledged dependence below, when I discuss Irigaray's reading of the fundamental role of the maternal in secretly grounding his metaphysics.

Aristotle does present a number of modalities of opposition that do not conform to binary structure. For instance, correlative oppositions are not binaries. They express a quantitative relation between terms, such as the double of a sum (6a36–b1). Both the double and the original sum have specific identities, which are not obviously hierarchical. Perhaps one could argue that the double is subordinate to the figure from which it is posited because the original sum must be articulated first in order for the double to have meaning. Even so, a hierarchy of this kind cannot be reduced to a binary opposition, because in a binary the devalorized term is identified only as the negation of its privileged opposite. In contrast, a figure posited in relation to another sum has a particular identity: a double is two times a unit.

There is no question that Aristotle figures possessions and privations hierarchically. For instance, in the *Categories*, blindness is presented as the absence of sight (12a26–28). Here, privation designates a specific and circumscribable lack. We would not speak of moles as blind because "healthy" animals in this species do not have eyes. The privation of sight, then, is predicated only of animals that lack a capacity others in his or her species possess. If privation designates a specific absence it does not, strictly speaking, fit into the A/Not-A relation found in a binary opposition, because the devalorized side of a binary is characterized by the infinitation of the negative. While Aristotle's formulation of possessions and privations in the *Categories* does not conform to a binary structure, his use of privation is looser elsewhere in his oeuvre. Aristotle acknowledges that his use of privation is broad. As he says in the *Metaphysics*, "There are just as many kinds of privations as there are words with negative prefixes" (1022b33–4).

In the *Categories* oppositions of contrariety take two forms. First, there are contrarieties that allow middle terms between them, such as white and black. For instance, all of the colors on the spectrum between white and black are "intermediates" (*metaxu* or *ana meson*) (12a17–20). Second, there are oppositions of contrariety such as health and sickness that admit no intermediates (12a1–10). In both cases, the opposed terms are conferred with specific identities that can be symbolized as an A/B relation. Yet Aristotle regularly renders all contrarieties as binary oppositions. Why? Intermediates tend to dissolve into a dualism, because a middle term is readily assimilated to one side or other of an opposition (Derrida 1981, 43). And Aristotle regards all dichotomies as hierarchical. One side is positive, while its other is a mere negative (G. E. R. Lloyd 1966, 65; Jay 1981, 46). For example, in the oppositions of white/black and man/woman, the first term is privileged over its "opposite." Significantly, both of the devalued terms named here—"black" and "woman"—become entangled with one another in Aristotle's discourse. The confusion of these terms occurs because they are thought only in relation to their privileged "opposites" and denied specific contours. Paradoxically, by neglecting to circumscribe these terms in his philosophy, Aristotle grants them an omnipotent status. For example, Irigaray argues that woman is not situated, which means, ironically, that she is more or less everywhere (Irigaray IR, 169–71/E, 17–8).

Jacques Derrida argues that the very nature of an opposition between two terms is tied to binary structure. This is why Derrida is wary of acknowledging "two" sexes. In his view, the figuration of two sexes tends to be structured according to the violent subordinating logic of (binary) dualism. For Derrida, man/woman is a hierarchical relation as long as it remains bound to the number "two."[4] Irigaray contends that binary oppositions do not involve *two* terms but *one* term (man) and its negated other (woman), and this second term, as I have said, has no identity specific to itself. This is one of the senses implied by her famous designation of woman as the sex that is Not-One (TS/CS).[5] But first, how does Aristotle conceive of difference?

THE SUBORDINATION OF DIFFERENCE TO IDENTITY

In a move that many twentieth-century philosophers decry, Aristotle defines difference in subordination to the concept of identity. Indeed, as Martin Heidegger, Derrida, Gilles Deleuze, Bergson, and Irigaray have argued, the act of defining difference in these terms obscures the very possibility of thinking difference.[6] For Irigaray, privileging identity over difference is the phallomorphic gesture par excellence. According to her argument, Aristotle's figuration of identity is established in unconscious homage to the erect penis. This maneuver jettisons feminine sexuality, along with the thinking of difference, to theoretical oblivion.[7]

And yet, Aristotle's position on the relation of difference and identity is by no means straightforward. In fact, there are tensions in his argument. There are in his discourse loci where difference emerges as nothing other than identity's enabling condition. Aristotle's project does not assimilate these moments of tension inhabiting his philosophy. But whether or not his system acknowledges these tensions is less important than their inscription in his oeuvre. Their legibility in his discourse is one of the reasons why Aristotle's texts are so fascinating, not only to scholars interested in the history of difference in metaphysics but to the future of thought and to the future of thinking sexual difference.

In *Metaphysics* 5,[8] Aristotle defines difference (*diaphora*) in the following terms:

> (1) those things which though other [*hetera*] are the same [*to auto*] in some respect, only not in number but either in species [*eidei*] or in genus [*genei*] or by analogy; (2) those whose genus is other [*heteron*], and contraries, and all things that have their otherness [*heterotēta*] in their substance [*ousia*]. (*Metaphysics* 5.1018a12–14)

In the first instance, he specifies that difference must be understood on the basis of a more primordial sameness (*to auto*). Thus, man and woman are both of the same species-form (*eidei*) but different in respect of their sex, black and white are contraries and yet both are predicated of the genus of color, and a trumpet blast and the color scarlet are different, while they are both analogously "loud." Second, Aristotle outlines an order of difference where there is generic otherness between two things. So, for example, Agamemnon's act of sacrificing Iphigenia is different to a clock.[9]

While Aristotle does not entirely abandon the formulation of difference presented in *Metaphysics* 5, he circumscribes a more specific conception of difference by distinguishing it from otherness (*allo*) in *Metaphysics* 10. In this treatise, he declares that all existent things are either other or the same, and otherness does not depend on identity. In contrast, difference is properly spoken of on the basis of a primordial sameness.

> But difference is not the same as otherness [*allo*]. For the other [*heteron*] and that from which it is other [*heteron*] than need not be other [*heteron*] in some definite respect [for everything that exists is either other or the same), but that which is different [*diaphora*] from anything is different *in some respect*, so that there must be *something identical* [*to auto*] whereby they differ. [My emphases] (*Metaphysics* 5:1054b23–26)

Here, Aristotle insists that difference properly so called presupposes a relation of *identity* or *sameness* (*to auto*). As I said a moment ago, identity can be spoken of in three ways: in terms of species, genus, or analogy. While in *Metaphysics* 5 Aristotle includes otherness in genus as a modality of difference, in this passage otherness in genus is excluded as a form of difference. For Aristotle, things that are merely other cannot be described as different, because they are too far distant from one another and have no point of comparison (1055a6–7). Thus, in *Metaphysics* 10, difference necessarily implies measurability and comparability, which can occur only if different things share a primary relation of sameness.[10]

Once Aristotle has established the primacy of identity (*to auto*) in defining difference in *Metaphysics* 10, he is able to specify what kind of difference is the "greatest" (*megistē*). He contends that contrariety is the greatest difference. This difference is greatest because it distinguishes the extremes from which the generation of species (*eidos*) take place (1055a5–15). While he does not deny that differences arise within species (for example, the distinction between a black and a white cat is a kind of difference), contrariety is a more important form of difference because it enables the emergence of distinct species.[11] Things that differ in genus are not comparable, and this means that they fall outside the limits of greatest difference.[12]

The privilege that Aristotle grants to contrariety, as the greatest difference in *Metaphysics* 10, must be understood in relation to his preoccupation with establishing the definition of his highest category of being, substance (*ousia*), in *Metaphysics* 7, which, as Jonathon Lear's helpful analysis makes clear, is the species-form (*eidos*) (286–87).[13] Differentia and genus do not exist as independent elements apart from the species-form. In other words, they have actuality only *through* the form (*eidos*), which is defined as one (*en*) in being (1037b25–28; 1038a5–8; Lear, 1988 286–7). To arrive at the species-form, the metaphysician must begin with the genus and divide it into differentia. This process does not stop with the division of the genus into differentia; the differentia must, in turn, be divided into further differentia, until the differentia can no longer be divided. For example, "endowed with feet" is a differentia of the genus "animal," but this is not sufficient to define a species, because the metaphysician must know the differentia of animal *qua* endowed with feet. In the next step, endowed with feet must be divided into cloven-footed and not-cloven-footed. To define a species, the process of division must continue until there are no more differences to be distinguished. In this instance, there are as many species of animal as there are differentiae of footedness. Aristotle thus designates the final differentia as the substantial form (*eidos*) (1038a9–24).

The preoccupation with the actuality of the species-form in the *Metaphysics* leads Aristotle to neglect the generative power of difference. As Deleuze remarks, the differentia of the differentia, which receives such careful attention in *Metaphysics* 7, merely names a kind of "false transport" (Deleuze 1994, 32). The *process* of differentiation is not studied as such, difference is thought only in terms of its role in establishing the identity of substance. In other words, Aristotle does not engage in thinking through *what difference does* prior to and in excess of the static concepts of genus and species-form.

In the foregoing discussion, I argued that Aristotle subordinates the thinking of difference to securing a definition for his highest category of being, substance, which occurs within the genus through the division of differentia. This hierarchical figuration of identity and difference is not sexually neutral. In Irigaray's terms, it amounts to the occlusion of the possibility of thinking *sexual* difference. The confinement of difference within the identity of the genus, however, cannot be considered definitive. Aristotle does allow for generic difference in *Metaphysics* 5. In another passage Deleuze has emphasized, Aristotle affirms that difference itself *has being* (998b22–23). For Deleuze, this claim amounts to a fracture in Aristotle's overall system. If difference has being, it cannot be housed safely within the walls of identity. It must be thought beyond the genus, that is, beyond any categorical determination (Deleuze 1994, 32). But Aristotle does not assimilate the implications of this fleeting assertion and claims in the same sentence that no genus can be predicated of its differentia.[14]

Irigaray also discerns loci of tension in Aristotle's engagement with identity and difference. She finds traces of the female sex that cannot be domesticated within the walls of his conceptual logic. At the end of this chapter, I contend that Irigaray finds that his texts tend to confuse difference—the interval—with woman.

PHYSIS

Irigaray's reading of Aristotle's *physis* emphasizes the sexuate stakes of his argument. *Physis* consists of form (*eidos, morphē*), a concept related explicitly to the male, and of matter (*hylē*), a concept related explicitly to the female. The relation of these two terms is not neutral; for Aristotle, form has privilege over matter. This hierarchy is infamous in feminist philosophy and has been subject to a number of critiques.[15] For my purposes, Irigaray's reading of the misogynist figuration of matter and form is particularly interesting. She manages to exploit the unthought excesses of this violent relation in order to subvert the way in which *physis* is understood.

In her first essay on Aristotle, Irigaray finds that his discourse seeps beyond its own protocols to reveal irreducible traces of alterity that cannot be subsumed into the hierarchical framework governing his thinking on *physis*. In her argument, these are traces of the maternal-feminine. For Irigaray, the maternal-feminine is not merely the denigrated other of Aristotle's valorized understanding of masculinity; on the contrary, the maternal-feminine is the name for a formulation that precedes and exceeds Aristotle's metaphysics. The maternal-feminine is unthinkable within the horizon of his masculine–feminine hierarchy.

It is not until Irigaray's introductory essay in *An Ethics of Sexual Difference* and her reading of *Physics* 4, "Place, Interval" in the same book, that *physis* is radically transformed. In these texts, she no longer refers to *physis* but to "nature" (*la nature*), and, in her discourse, "nature" implies that between matter and form there is a sexed relationship that is nonhierarchical.

While Irigaray's critique of the sexed hierarchy embedded in Aristotle's presentation of *physis* is well documented, I do not believe the importance of her transformative elaboration of *physis*, matter, and form has received sufficient scholarly attention.[16] In my view, tracing Aristotle's thesis on *physis* and the evolution of Irigaray's discourse on this thesis is vital to appreciating the complexity of her engagement with his thinking.

What is Aristotle's position on *physis*? He declares that *physis* in the primary and strict sense is the substance (*ousia*) of things which have in themselves a source (*archēn*) of movement (*kinēsis*) and of rest (*stasis*). In contrast, artificial products do not contain a principle of movement and rest, which means they have no innate impulse to change (*kinēsis*) (192b14–22; 1015a13–15). For Aristotle, "this suggests that nature [*physis*] is a sort of source and cause [*aitios*] of change and remaining unchanged in that to which it belongs primarily and of itself" (192b21).[17]

In order to account for *physis*, he must define its inherent capacity for movement. He does this by drawing on the contrasts and similarities between things that exist by *physis* and artifacts that, to come into being, require the action of something external.

In a characteristic gesture, Aristotle draws on the work of his predecessors to elaborate his own argument. He notes that some writers identify the substance (*ousia*) of *physis* with matter (*hylē*) while others understand it as the form (*morphē, eidos*) (193a29–31). Antiphon is named as a representative of the first position. According to Aristotle's predecessor, if a bed was left to rot and a shoot sprang up from it, it would be wood that grows from the bed, not bed from bed (193a12–16).[18] In Antiphon's argument, this shows that matter persists throughout the bed's production and decay, whereas the art (*technē*) that arranged the bed (i.e., its form) is merely an accidental attribute. Thus, for Antiphon, matter is the bed's substance.

In contrast to Antiphon, Aristotle regards wood as the potential (*dynamis*) for the bed. More broadly, this is how he understands matter: it is the primary underlying substrate (*hypokeimenon*) of each thing (192a31). It functions as the potential for a thing to become a substance but cannot be said to actually exist (*entelechia*). In order for a thing to claim the status of substance in actuality (*entelechia*), it must have form (*morphē, eidos*). This is not to say that matter passes away with the emergence of form; Aristotle, like Antiphon, affirms that matter persists throughout the emergence and decay of things that come to be by *physis*. But it is the presence of form with matter that defines *physis,* and, when form is absent, substance is merely potential. He demonstrates his argument in a famous analogy. In the same way that wood is the substrate for a bed, in things constituted by *physis*

> that which is flesh or bone only in possibility [*dynamin*], before it acquires the form [*eidos*] which accords with the account by which we define [*ton logon*] what flesh or bone is, does not yet have its proper nature [*physis*] and is not a thing due to nature. So there is another way of speaking [*ton logon*], according to which nature is the shape and form of things which have in themselves a source of their changes [*kinēseōs archēn e morphē kai to eidos*].[19] (*Physics* 4.193a35–b4)

In this passage, Aristotle affirms that form is the proper source, of movement and of rest, that defines *physis* as what it is. This is manifest in the *Parts of Animals*, where he asserts that the *physis* of an animal is a first principle (*archē*) rather than its matter (642a17). What establishes form's priority over matter is the distinction between potentiality (*dynamis*) and actuality (*entelechia*). He writes: "The form has a better claim than the matter to be called nature [*physis*]. For we call a thing something, when it is that thing in actuality [*entelechia*], rather than just in possibility [*dynamis*]" (193b7–8).[20]

In Aristotle's terms, the intelligible order actualized by form (*eidos*) is divine. The deity (*theos*) is the highest being in his metaphysics, and it is the only being uncontaminated by matter and occupying no place (*topos*). In other words, the deity is pure actuality (*entelechia*) and does not suffer the changes and destructions characteristic of artifacts and things that come to be by *physis*.[21] Form's divine status, then, is conferred because, like the deity, it is characterized as actuality (*entelechia*).

Aristotle conceives of the emergence of things due to *physis* as a kind of destruction (*phthora*) (192a20). In his view, form annihilates its contrary in order to come into being. But matter cannot be destroyed in this process, because, as we know, it persists with form in defining the substance of *physis*, albeit in a subordinate role. What is destroyed? For Aristotle, it is lack or privation (*sterēsis*) that form destroys. And matter is characterized by privation before it has acquired form—although my phrasing here deserves qualification; strictly speaking, matter and privation are two different things. They do not belong together, except, Aristotle says, by virtue of concurrence (*symbebēkos*) (192a4–5). He distinguishes privation and matter, then, because the latter as potentiality is nearly a substance, while privation has no claim to substantial existence; it is an absence of being. It would seem that matter, in Aristotle's account of *physis*, is not characterized by lack in any necessary respect. For Irigaray, however, matter and lack are intimately entwined in Aristotle's corpus. Moreover, this intimate relationship between the primary substrate and privation has decisive consequences for woman and for the possibility of thinking the interval.

It sounds paradoxical to describe the emergence of things that come to be by *physis* as a kind of destruction. Aristotle's reasoning is demanded by his commitment to the law of noncontradiction. This axiom was discussed earlier; it holds that "the same attribute cannot at the same time belong and not-belong in the same subject in the same respect" (1005a20). In this sense, form must destroy privation, because the simultaneous presence of these opposites with the underlying substrate would violate what he regards as the most certain of all axioms.

Aristotle uses "privation" (*sterēsis*) in a number of ways. Sometimes it is restricted to demarcating a specific "lack," such as blindness, while in other places it is vaguer, notably in the *Metaphysics*, where he says there are as many kinds of privations as there are words with negative prefixes (1022b33). In the context of defining things that come to be by *physis*, he goes so far as to describe privation as an evil tendency (*kakopoiein*). It is clearly denigrated, then, whereas matter, while devoid of specific qualities, has at least a claim to potential existence (192a15). And yet privation has a more definite identity than matter. Once Aristotle has argued for form's privilege in defining things that come to be by *physis*, he suggests that things can be called *physis* and form (*morphē*) in two ways. In addition to using form as the name of the concept that defines the substance of things, he says that privation can be understood as form in the sense that it designates a specific state, that of absence (193b19). Matter, on the other hand, is merely an underlying substrate that has the capacity to "not-be" when privation abides with it and "to-be" once it has acquired form.

For Irigaray, the denial of any particularities to matter is significant. She contends that its figuration as the substrate of substance is an act that betrays philosophy's dependence on the maternal debt.

> And, what of the "first matter"? This unknowable, which does not possess an existence in itself, what is it? That which eludes the question of *tode di*, might it not be the becoming body of/in the mother? The becoming *physis* always already constituted as *hypokeimenon* for the definition of the substance of Man. [Translation modified] (S, 161/SA, 201)

In this passage, Irigaray emphasizes that matter is never considered in itself. Indeed, Aristotle makes this claim precisely, thereby placing an interdiction on any attempt to think through materiality in excess of its capacity to receive both form and the privation of form (1036a8).[22] Irigaray's attribution of maternal status to *hylē* is not simply a projection of her interests into his corpus. Nor is the association of man with substance (*ousia*) imposed without reference to his texts. He explicitly relates matter to woman in his oeuvre, while form and, by implication, substance are linked to man. This relation is complicated by the fact that he also associates privation with woman metaphorically.

Whether what comes to be is due to *physis* or to *tekhnē*, Aristotle thinks of the process of becoming in terms of desire (*orexis*). It cannot be form that desires, because it is not defective, and it cannot be privation that yearns for transformation, because then it would desire its own destruction. For Aristotle, it is matter that desires actualization. At the exact moment that matter is presented as defective—because it is merely a potential substance, characterized by privation—it is related to the feminine. "You might say that it [matter] yearns [*oregētai*] as the female for the male and as the base for the beautiful; except that it is neither base nor female, except by virtue of concurrence" (*symbebēkos*) (192a16–23).[23] Here, "beautiful" (*kalos*) and "male" (*arren*) are metaphors for form. And "base" (*aiskhron*) and "female" (*thēlu*) are not ascribed to matter as such; they function as metaphors for the privation characteristic of matter before it has acquired form. As I have emphasized, matter is devoid of qualities. Desire, then, cannot be proper to matter. It is attributed to the substrate only by virtue of its concurrence (*symbebēkos*) with privation.[24]

Regardless of whether desire is interpreted in this passage as proceeding from the deity's will or from the primary substrate, the metaphors of "female" and "base" are inextricably linked together and opposed to "male" and "beauty." When matter does acquire form, its female and base characteristics are destroyed. In this context, the female sex is figured as privation, which the male principle overcomes through destruction.

For Aristotle, the substance of *physis*—form—has a masculine connotation. In the common parlance of his contemporaries, *physis* was slang for genitals in human beings, and *physis* was particularly associated with women's genitals (Winkler 1990, 217–20). This is presumably the case because, as Francis Cornford points out, the word *physein* in ancient Greek meant "to give birth to" (Cornford 1952, 181).

But Aristotle did not follow the popular discourse of the day. If females were allowed any privileged share in the substance of *physis*, the hierarchical distribution of form, matter, and privation would unravel.

It might be objected here that the designations of privation as "female" and form as "male" are metaphoric. After all, Aristotle regards metaphor as "obscure" (*asaphes*) in philosophy and secondary to the "clarity" (*saphes*) of definition (97b37–39). On this line of reasoning, Aristotle's metaphors are mere ornaments that might be substituted for other metaphors or dispensed with in a more exact presentation of his concepts. For Irigaray, the detour into obscurity that metaphor enacts is essential to the clarity of definition. In other words, the metaphors bound up in Aristotle's conceptual architecture cannot be substituted for other metaphors or discarded in order to articulate a "purely" conceptual framework. His philosophy is constituted through a complex interplay of hierarchically sexed concept-metaphors.[25]

"THE FORM OF THE HUMAN IS HIS NATURE"

If female functions as a metaphor for privation in the *Physics*, in *The Generation of Animals* female is identified with matter.[26] Form is again associated with the male sex. Irigaray exploits the shift in Aristotle's text between associating *female* with privation in one instance and with matter in another. The fact that his use of *female* is fluid within his discourse allows Irigaray to render what she calls the maternal-feminine a subversive concept. More precisely, for Irigaray, the maternal-feminine is not a concept; she is the very condition of conceptual logic. And because her contours are uncircumscribed, Irigaray can move beyond the strictures of the infamous law of noncontradiction. The maternal-feminine is both privation *and* matter, and yet she is also *not* privation *and* matter. On the one hand, she does not exist, and on the other hand, Irigaray discerns traces of her in many places in Aristotle's discourse.

One of the ways Aristotle establishes a hierarchical relationship between man and woman is through the classification of semen (*sperma*) and menstrual fluid (*katamenia*). Semen provides what he calls the moving cause and is analogous to a tool. Menstrual fluid, on the other hand, is classed as prime matter (*prōte hylē*).

> For the menstrual blood is semen not in a pure state but in need of working up, just as in the formation of fruits the nutriment is present, when it is not yet sifted thoroughly, but needs working up to purify it. Thus the menstrual blood causes generation by mixture with the semen, as this impure nutriment in plants is nutritious when mixed with pure nutriment. (*Generation of Animals* 728a26–30)

Semen is "pure" (*katharon*), while menstrual blood needs "working up" (*ergasias*) to be purified. Menstrual blood is a modality of matter—indeed, it is an exemplary modality given that it is classified as prime matter (*prōte hylē*). Aristotle does not dwell on the perplexing status of menstrual fluid as the first matter. As the underlying substrate (*hypokeimenon*), it is a necessary condition for life, and in this sense it has at least temporal priority over semen. Nonetheless, by designating menstrual fluid as impure in opposition to the purity of semen, he ensures that the former is rendered deficient to the latter. In short, semen does the creative work of generation, while menstrual fluid provides the matter for this work (727b31–33; 729a9–11). Menstrual fluid, then, is necessary to the process of generation, but the action comes from the male source, the semen.

That semen is itself an order of matter is both acknowledged and denied in the *Generation of Animals*. Like menstrual fluid, semen is regarded as a residue of digestive material, and in this sense it is considered material. In another sense, however, semen is designated as immaterial and related to the deity. This divine aspect of semen has soul (*psychē*) potentially and contributes what is called the intellect (*nous*) to the embryo in the process of insemination (737a7–10). In contrast, menstrual fluids have all the parts of the embryo potentially *except* for the divine principle. For Aristotle, "the female is, as it were, a mutilated male [*arren esti pepiromenon*], and the menstrual fluids are semen, only not pure; for there is only one thing they have not in them, the principle of soul" (737a27–29). Menstrual fluids are thus confined to the realm of sensibility, while the privileged aspect of semen transcends matter; it is divine. What about the material aspect of semen? Aristotle tells us it is a watery substance that dissolves and evaporates, which means that no part of it contributes to the generation of the embryo (737a11). The aspect of semen that gives potential soul to human being and what is unique to "him"—intellect—is not contaminated by the transitory world of the body. Conveniently, because the material part of semen evaporates, the female sex becomes the exclusive bearer of matter in the process of generation.[27]

Aristotle classifies semen as the moving cause in the reproduction of animals. The moving cause is one of four causes in his doctrine of causality. Two of the four causes—matter and form—have already been discussed. In this context, they are known respectively as the primary substrate and the efficient cause. The third and fourth causes are the moving cause and final cause. In sexual reproduction, matter (i.e., menstrual fluid) comes from the female parent. The form comes from the male; it is the shape (*morphē*) of man, often described by Aristotle according to the stock definition of his day: rational, two-legged animal. The moving cause also comes from the male parent and is the semen. The final cause is the "perfect fully-grown man" (Lloyd AGS, 59–60).[28]

There are several points to be emphasized here. Three of the four causes in reproduction are explicitly rendered masculine. Only one, matter, is feminine, and Aristotle often juxtaposes matter to the other three causes taken together (Lloyd AGS, 60; Lear 1989, 28). The female sex is almost entirely shut out of the process of change. And the cause that does have a feminine connotation is abstract stuff that cannot even claim the status of substance without the intervention of the three masculine causes.

Another point to note is that the explicit goal of sexual generation is the production of a man. As Jay has argued, females are figured in Aristotle's thought as monstrosities (1981, 46). Irigaray agrees. Aristotle theorizes the conception of a girl as an aberration or monstrosity (S 209/SA, 167). For Aristotle, when the proper amount of vital heat is present in the male's sperm, a boy is engendered, and it is only when there is insufficient vital heat in the sperm that a girl is conceived (766b15–25). An adult woman is also monstrous. In a notorious passage, Aristotle writes: "Now a boy is like a woman in form, and the woman is as it were an impotent [*adynamia*] male, for it is through a certain incapacity that the female is female, being incapable of concocting the nutriment in its last stage into semen" (728a16–21). For him, woman is a failed or lesser man because her menstrual fluid, unlike the divine aspect of semen, cannot transcend materiality.[29]

The inferiority of the female to the male is not confined to humans. In a castrated animal its *whole form* is transformed to such an extent that it seems to be "female or not far short of it" (716b5–9). In this context, the female is figured as an animal deprived of a sex. This absence, or her "incapacity" (*adynamin*), is presented as the privation of the organs that produce semen to beget a new animal.[30] On the other hand, the female sex is not without her usefulness. She furnishes the process of generation with matter and she also provides a "place" (*topōn*) for the growing embryo in her womb (726a34–b1). Aristotle manifestly regards these functions as less significant than the male contributions to reproduction. The womb does not figure as a cause in his schema, and the substratum is "impotent" (*adynamin*) without the action of the three masculine causes.

To the extent that Aristotle acknowledges woman's role in sexual generation, he downplays her contributions. For instance, in the course of elaborating his doctrine of causality in the *Metaphysics*, he names the father as an example of the *source of change* or the moving cause of his child, but when he describes the primary substratum he omits mentioning the role of the mother (1013a24–33). In the *Physics*, after establishing the form or shape (*eidos*, *morphē*) as the essence of *physis*, he concludes: "If the shape [*morphē*] is art, then on the same principle the shape of the human is nature [*physis*]. For human is born from human [*gignetai gar ex anthrōpoi anthrōpōs*]" (translation modified, 193b12). This turn of phrase ignores woman's contribution to reproduction altogether.

WOMAN-MATTER AND THE MATERNAL-FEMININE

In "How to Conceive (of) a Girl?" Irigaray argues that matter and woman are indistinguishable in Aristotle because they are uncircumscribed within his conceptual framework. The confusion of woman-matter has extraordinary implications for metaphysics and for the future of thinking sexual difference.

First, a word on the shifting senses in which Irigaray inscribes "woman" and the "feminine." The status of these words in her texts has generated considerable controversy in feminist scholarship. Many theorists accused her of reifying a biologically determinist conception of "woman" and the "feminine." As Chanter argues, the attribution of essentialism to Irigaray overlooks the fact that she engages with woman and the feminine precisely in order to call into question the oppositions (biology/culture, sex/gender) through which these words have been typically understood. Her texts do not affirm reductive biologism, nor do they put "woman" and the "feminine" into free play as signs that have no particular relation to women. Irigaray's use of "nature," "the feminine," and "woman" does not conform to the violent cleavages of these oppositions. Instead, she inscribes these words in ways that displace the functioning of the dichotomies between sex and gender and between nature and culture (Chanter EE, 21–46).[31]

Irigaray's essay "How to Conceive (of) a Girl?" draws heavily on Aristotle's theses on *physis* and sexual generation. In the course of describing the role of the concepts of woman and the female sex in his discourse, she deploys these concepts in the denigrated and misogynist framework of his thinking. Yet this is not strictly true. Irigaray's description is punctuated with questions to Aristotle and interjections into his text that disrupt the functioning of his conceptual apparatus. Her reading of his texts reveals that woman and the female sex exceed the terms of his logic. How?

The status of woman and the female sex oscillate in Aristotle's texts—her sex is construed as the impotence (*adynamin*) of the male in one context, while her menstrual fluids are also begrudgingly acknowledged as one of the four causes (*prōte hylē*). Her womb functions as a *topos* for the growing embryo, although the womb is not granted the status of a cause, while in the *Physics* "female" is related to "base" or "ugly" (*kakopoiein*) and is construed as a metaphor for the privation (*stēresis*) of substance. Woman has an especially strong affinity with matter. For example, when a female is described as a mutilated male (*arren esti pepiromenon*), her mutilation is affirmed because her menstrual fluid lacks the ability to transmit soul, a suprasensible and divine substance. In other words, menstrual fluid is construed as lacking because it is confined to the realm of materiality (728a26–30; 726a34–b1; 192a14–23; 737a27–29).

For Irigaray, woman and materiality are indistinguishable in Aristotle. This might seem like a significant sleight of hand to some of Aristotle's readers. I do not believe, however, that this is the case. He presents matter as undefinable; it has no qualities peculiar to itself. The most that can be said of materiality is that it functions as the underlying substrate (*hypokeimenon*) on which form or privation impresses qualitative specificity (1036a8; 192a31). My discussion of Aristotle's theory of sexual generation emphasized his inability to consider the particular contributions of the female parent. The mother is always looked at with reference to the privileged yardstick of the male sex and she is found wanting. To the extent that she is identified with anything, she is aligned with matter. Irigaray's interchangeable inscriptions of "first matter," *hylē*, *hypokeimenon,* and "woman," then, are drawn from Aristotle's argument (S, 161, 162/SA, 201, 202).

According to Irigaray's reading, matter, woman, and the female sex are concepts without substantial value or definition. In contrast, the masculine concepts of form, moving cause, final cause, and substance are privileged. Irigaray detects an isomorphic congruence between the elevation of these clearly circumscribed masculine concepts and the phallocentric representation of the male sex (S, 161/SA, 201). She argues that Aristotle's denigrated presentation of the female sex, woman, and matter figures these "concepts" as domesticated by their privileged masculine contraries. "Matter-potency [*matière-puissance*] is duly corseted in/by rigid categories" (S, 163/SA, 204). She is assigned a formless status, which she cannot exceed. Woman-matter is figured as "other of the same"—that is, as the absence of the masculine causes, rather than as genuinely different and irreducible to her phallomorphic opposites (Irigaray 2000, 123–24).[32]

Yet Irigaray's description of Aristotle demonstrates that woman and matter are much more than the colonized substrates that the masculine causes work up in order to engender substances. Paradoxically, it is the amorphic status assigned to her that renders woman-matter uncontainable within his system. This is evident in the following passage, where Irigaray's iteration of Aristotelian "woman" (*gynos*, *la femme*) embraces materiality and the female sex:

> Woman, for her part, remains in unrealised potentiality [*la puissance*] —unrealised, at least, for/by herself. *Is she, by nature, a being that exists for/by another?* And in her share of substance, not only is she secondary to man but she may just as well not be as be. Ontological status makes her incomplete and uncompletable. She can *never* achieve the *wholeness* of her form. Or perhaps her form has to be seen—paradoxically—as mere *privation*? But this question can never be decided since woman is never resolved by/in being, but remains the simultaneous co-existence of opposites. She is *both one and the other*. . . . She is equally *neither one nor the other*. (S 165/SA, 206)

This passage is elaborated with close reference to Aristotle's theories of sexual generation and of things that come to be by *physis*. By posing questions that he does not ask, Irigaray's reading makes explicit the paradoxical, even contradictory status of woman-matter within his argument. She is both privation (*stērēsis*) and potentiality (*dynamis*) and she is equally *neither one nor the other*. Woman-matter violates Aristotle's most certain principle of logic, the law of noncontradiction. She is a threat to the very constitution of his philosophy.

In accordance with his views, Irigaray presents woman and matter as denigrated concepts. But, as the passage I have just quoted demonstrates, Irigaray's inscription of woman-matter draws out her excessiveness, her fluidity. In the descriptive moments of Irigaray's writing, then, the iteration of woman (and indeed of matter, the female sex, and the feminine) is never simply a confirmation of the secondary and debased status Aristotle attributes to her. Her texts reveal woman-matter as a subversive figure within phallocentric discourse. She cannot be contained as the other (of the same) masculine causes. She exceeds the order of concepts; she cannot even be resolved to be or not to be.

Woman-matter's contradictory status is pregnant with disavowed meaning. In Irigaray's terms, woman-matter—or *hylē*, *hypokeimenon*, the female sex (*thēlu*), and woman (*gynos*)—are traces of what she calls the maternal-feminine, the obscured ground of metaphysics. Where woman-matter is merely the other of the phallocentric figuration of man, the maternal-feminine is irreducibly other to metaphysics.

The maternal-feminine cannot appear within Aristotle's discourse, since his thinking is predicated on her exclusion. Nonetheless, the burial of the maternal-feminine has left traces within his philosophy, which are discernable in the contradictory figurations of woman-matter.

The dependence of metaphysics on the maternal-feminine is difficult to discern in Aristotle's texts, because his depictions of *hylē, hypokeimenon*, woman, and the female sex are consistently derogatory. Yet this is perhaps symptomatic of a denial or a refusal of awareness of the unseverable relation between metaphysics and the mother-matter (*la mère-matière*) (S, 162/SA, 202). In other words, Aristotle's misogynist assessments of woman-matter can be interpreted as unconscious maneuvers of defense to protect his system of thought from the dangers of its relation to the maternal-feminine.

More broadly, Irigaray says his philosophy is "always already rigged" (*toujours déjà truqués*) to obfuscate the relation to the maternal-feminine (S, 162/SA, 202). In order to make this foundational dependence explicit, Irigaray is obliged to install the mother within his discourse. This is an act of insinuation because, as I have argued, the maternal-feminine cannot appear within metaphysics. Irigaray does this by suggesting that the first matter (*la matière première, prōte hylē*) in the emergence of *physis* is the body of the mother. And she takes issue with Aristotle by crediting the mother as the primary source of *physis* (S, 161/SA, 201). This particular gesture is, of course, grossly improper for a rigorous Aristotelian, given that the master explicitly teaches that the primary source (*prōte archēn*) of *physis* is substance (*ousia*), the divine masculine concept of form.

I alluded earlier to the concept of the deity, the highest principle in Aristotle's metaphysics. He elevates this Unbegotten Being beyond the realm of matter and place; the deity is pure actuality (*entelechia*). Irigaray describes the deity as the "absolute (self)principle" (S, 161/SA, 201). In other words, she discerns an isomorphic relation between Aristotle's deity and the phallocentric figuration of man. For Irigaray, the Unbegotten Being is secretly dependent on the maternal-feminine. She writes, "'First matter' . . . is perhaps the foundation upon which the supreme elevation (of) god is erected" (S, 161–2/SA, 202).

In this early essay, then, Irigaray challenges the hierarchical distributions at work in Aristotle's system. Instead of allowing the deity to stand as the highest principle of his metaphysics and cosmology, she argues that the maternal-feminine is the disavowed ground on which his project is built. This has decisive consequences for the matter–form relation. The divine privilege of form is displaced by the priority of mother-matter and is identified as the primary source of *physis*. This maneuver subverts the hierarchical distributions of his system. But this step does not constitute a rejection of Aristotle's thinking. On the contrary, Irigaray's emphasis on the maternal-feminine as the obscure foundation of his project is intimately engaged with his philosophy, and, by making the sexuate stakes of his metaphysics explicit, she prepares for the possibility of thinking sexual difference in relation to his project.

In a sense, Irigaray's reading of Aristotle already describes sexual difference. The relation between the maternal-feminine substrate and phallocentric metaphysics is a sexed relation. This is not, however, the order of sexual difference that Irigaray wants to affirm, since it is violently hierarchical and institutes philosophy on the effacement of the maternal-feminine. It is a binary figuration, where the phallic concepts of metaphysics achieve divine and ideal definition (A), while the maternal-feminine is construed as formless fluidity (Not-A). This demands qualification. In the process of diagnosing the foundational status of this phallocentric hierarchy in Aristotle, Irigaray demonstrates that the exclusion of the maternal-feminine fails. Woman is *both* privation and matter and she is equally *neither one nor the other* (S, 165/SA, 206). She violates the law of noncontradiction and confounds herself with being and not-being. In other words, the very gesture of describing Aristotle's phallocentrism collapses the A/Not-A opposition on which his philosophy is erected.

To break down the phallic/maternal-feminine, solid/fluid, form/formless dichotomies underwriting Aristotlean metaphysics is not enough to articulate feminine specificity beyond phallocentrism. To achieve this difficult task demands a rethinking of difference. Irigaray does not succeed in "How to Conceive of (a) Girl?" in positing a sexuate relation that is nonhierarchical. It is in "Place, Interval" and the introduction to *Ethics* that she articulates sexual difference in the radical sense. The threshold of this relation is the interval. While the interval is not yet the focus of Irigaray's attention in her first essay on Aristotle, she does develop a significant account of the hierarchically sexed connotations of difference in his thinking, and it is to these connotations that I turn in the final section.

THE PHALLOMORPHISM OF IDENTITY AND THE OBLIVION OF THE INTERVAL

Aristotle conceives of difference primarily in subordination to identity. This is particularly pronounced in *Metaphysics* 10, where difference is distinguished from otherness. For him, otherness does not require a relation of identity between two things, while difference is predicated on the basis of a primordial sameness. He stipulates that the "greatest" difference emerges from a common genus and secures the identity of the species-form (*eidos*). In this context, difference is privileged because it is the concept that divides the genus into differentia until no more divisions can be made. These divisions are attended to only insofar as they are necessary to the establishment of the species-form, which defines his conception of substance (*ousia*). Aristotle's preoccupation with the product of difference (the identity of substance) leads him to neglect the process of differentiation (1054b23–26, 1055a5–15).

And yet a number of oscillations were discerned in the *Metaphysics*. In a fascinating passage, Aristotle affirms that difference itself has being (998b22–23) and in *Metaphysics* 5 he allows difference to be predicated between things that are other in genus (1018a12–14). He does not, however, assimilate these fleeting assertions, which means his philosophy is overwhelmingly inclined to efface difference while privileging the identity of the concepts of genus and species.

For Irigaray, Aristotle's fixation on establishing the identity of the genus and the identity of the species-form are expressions of phallomorphism. In her terms, these clearly demarcated concepts are isomorphically congruent with the figuration of the penis as erect and singular. The consequences of elevating these phallic concepts are disastrous for the possibility of articulating sexual difference, since what is in excess in respect to form is the female sex (Irigaray

TS, 110–11/CS, 109). The submission of difference to the authority of identity excludes the possibility of thinking woman in her specificity, while instantiating a phallocentric theoretical framework.

To the extent that difference subsists in subordination to the privileged concepts of genus and species-form, woman appears as other in Aristotle's discourse. This otherness is not cognized as radically other, as irreducible to identity of the concept. She is thought as different only on the basis of a primordial sameness with man (the concept of species-form) (1058b21–25). Yet, following Irigaray, I have argued that Aristotle's figuration of woman is much more contradictory than he acknowledges. She seeps beyond her corseted role, confounding herself with matter *and* privation, being *and* not-being. In this sense, woman-matter cannot be contained within the concept of species-form (*eidos*) (S, 165/SA, 206).

I have suggested that woman's excessiveness is a trace of the maternal-feminine in Aristotle's metaphysics. This excessive status is also entangled with the interval of sexual difference. For Irigaray, the interval falls outside Aristotle's definition of sameness. In contrast to Deleuze, who also celebrates a concept of difference that precedes identity, Irigaray's figuration of the interval is sexed. The interval is the generative threshold differentiating the sexes, which articulates the masculine and feminine poles of life as irreducible. On Irigaray's argument, the interval is a figuration of difference in excess of identity; the interval is the very condition on which the identity of concepts is predicated (ESD/E).

Aristotle's phallocentric project is posited on the basis of the occlusion of a violent hierarchy that elevates his conception of philosophy while subordinating its effaced other: the maternal-feminine. Because this relation of dependence is not acknowledged, his metaphysics is presented as self-sufficient. The difference that obscures the maternal-feminine is the interval of sexual difference. In this context, the interval effaces "itself" in the movement of conceiving philosophy as phallocentrism. Nonetheless, the interval instantiates a *sexual* relation between the formless fluidity of the maternal-feminine and the phallocratic conceptual edifice that makes up Aristotle's metaphysics. Where Irigaray insists that radical sexual difference must be thought through the interval, Aristotle's project fails to cognize the grounding status of the interval. Aristotle's occlusion of the interval and the maternal-feminine renders them indistinguishable in his corpus. Yet neither the maternal-feminine nor the interval are *present* in his texts, so how can they flounder together in confusion?

I have distinguished a denigrated concept of woman in Aristotle from the maternal-feminine. Woman (*gynos*) appears in his discourse as, for example, an "impotent" (*adynamin*) male (728a16–21). In contrast, the maternal-feminine is not found *in* his work. But her effacement has left its marks in his discourse, as inscriptions of woman-matter. In this sense, Irigaray's reading of his work demonstrates that maintaining a strict distinction between these two "terms" is impossible because the contours of woman and the maternal-feminine are not circumscribed.

The maternal-feminine, in her very fluidity, also embraces the interval. An attentive reading of Aristotle's inscriptions of woman betrays traces of the maternal-feminine *and* the interval. Traces of woman's confusion with the interval are discernable in Aristotle in those places where woman exceeds her assigned role to oscillate between privation and matter. For instance, in a passage analyzed earlier in this chapter, Aristotle describes privation as an evil tendency (192a15). In the following paragraph, he compares the privative state of matter to the female sex (192a16–23). Charlton has argued that Aristotle regards privation as evil because it is unlimited and fluid (Aristotle 1970, 82). The connotations of evil infinity emanating from woman-matter here are traces of difference beyond the secure identity of the concepts of genus and species. These are traces of the interval of sexual difference. We can see from this example that the interval is not thought as such; instead, the interval is confused with a denigrated conception of woman-matter.

For Irigaray, the abyssal implications of the interval and the maternal-feminine lurking within Aristotle's woman-matter render her an extraordinarily dangerous figure to his metaphysics. Woman-matter's deprivation of contours makes her omnipotent; "because she is deprived of everything, "she" also wants to take possession of everything (*[elle] désire s'appropier (à) tout car elle est privation de tout*)" (S, 167/SA, 208).

Feminist theorists interested in thinking the female sex as something other than formless fluidity, as something other than a figure deprived of a sex (organ), will find little joy in woman's omnipotence. The female sex needs to be articulated with her own particularities. It is in this sense that Irigaray concludes "How to Conceive (of) a Girl?" pessimistically. Woman does not exist. The best that can be said is that she does not exist yet (S, 166/SA, 207). Here, Irigaray inscribes "woman" as a name for the female sex that is not denigrated. "Woman," in this sense, would be thought in her specificity. But how is "woman" cognizable, in Aristotelian discourse? In a famous interview, Irigaray says:

> Can female sexuality articulate itself, even minimally, within an Aristotelian type of logic? No. Within this logic, which dominates our most everyday statements—while speaking, at this moment, we are still observing its rules, female sexuality cannot articulate itself, unless precisely as an "undertone," a "lack," in discourse. But why would this situation be unchanging? Why can one not transcend that logic? To speak outside of it?(1981, 64)

Her call to move outside of Aristotle is by no means a naïve invocation to abandon his thought, as if this were even possible. On the contrary, to step beyond Aristotle is to maintain an intimate relation to his thinking, to draw out the paradoxes and blind spots lurking in his texts. But it is more than this. To speak outside of Aristotle is to articulate new values that enable the female sex to be thought in her specificity. Irigaray engages in this task by writing in the margins and silences of Aristotle's texts. In other words, Irigaray speaks "outside" of Aristotle by continuing to read him.

2. Being in Place

And (the most basic way of all) as [a thing is] in a vessel and, generally, in a place [*pantin de kuriōtaton to os en angeiōi kai olos en topōi*].

ARISTOTLE, *Physics* 4.210a24

THIS CHAPTER IS PARTICULARLY CONCERNED with the relationship between the concept of place (*topos*) and bodies that come to be by *physis*, a relationship elaborated in Aristotle's *Physics* 4.1–5. His concept of *topos* is irreducible to space and must be thought beyond mathematical calculation. Further, a deconstructive reading of the *Physics* suggests that *topos*—a sensible relation between two bodies that are different in being—has foundational status in Aristotle.[1] I argue that the relation between place and the body surrounded by place is the condition for the identity of substance (*ousia*), the primary category in his equivocal ontology (210a15–24; 1003a33). Aristotle does not assimilate the grounding status of being-in *topos*. This is a paradox that opens his project to an excess that is *other* than substance, a corporeal relation that cannot be reduced to identity.

TOPOS AS A CONCEPT IN EXCESS OF MATHEMATICAL CALCULATION

The primary motivation at work in Aristotle's interest in *topos* is to explain the concrete relations between bodies that come to be by *physis*. This distinguishes the study of *topos* from a mathematical investigation into the nature of space, because he believes that abstract space does not account for the specific relationships between bodies, as they exist in nature (*physis*).

Aristotle conceives of *physis* in the strict sense as the substance (*ousia*) of things that have in themselves a source (*archēn*) of movement (*kinēsis*) and of rest (*stasis*) (192b14–22). In order to define the concrete location of things that come to be by *physis*, he must establish a concept that has reference to motion. In fact, his belief in *topos* is demanded by his theory of locomotion (*phoran*), the most general kind (*koinē*) of movement. As he puts it, *topos* must exist because locomotion is defined as change (*kinēseōs*) of *topos* (208a31). Moreover, the locomotion of natural bodies (*physikōn sōmatōn*) would suggest that *topos* has some power (*dynamin*). When a body is not impeded it travels to its own place (*autōn topōn*). For instance, light bodies such as fire travel "above" (*anō*), while heavy bodies such as earth travel "below" (*katō*) (208b8–22). The fact that bodies are subject to locomotion, according to the Aristotle, is nothing less than the distinguishing feature of *topos* (211a12–13).

His interest in *topos* as a concept of physics is very different from the mathematical approach to space (*chōra*) articulated by geometers. Why? In contrast to *topos*, geometrical space is abstracted from the particularities of sensible bodies in their concrete environs (King 1950, 76–77; Duhem 1976a, 24–25; 1976b, 27–29). Let me turn to a difficult passage, from the second book of the *Physics*, that King has emphasized (193b23–194a1; King 1950, 77). Aristotle distinguishes mathematical knowledge from natural science. Both of these sciences are concerned with natural bodies that contain surfaces and volumes, and lines and points. Physics is interested in these bodies insofar as they exist in nature and this means they must be approached as bodies that contain within themselves a principle of motion. Mathematics, on the other hand, does not consider these bodies qua *physis*. Instead, it is concerned with bodies in abstraction from movement.

> Both the student of nature and the mathematician deal with these things [the limits of bodies]; but the mathematician does not consider them as boundaries of natural bodies. Nor does he consider things that supervene as supervening on such bodies. That is why he separates them; for they are separable in thought from change, and it makes no difference; no error results. Those who talk about ideas do

> not notice that they too do this: they separate physical things though they are less separable than the objects of mathematics.[2] (*Physics* 2.193b31–194a1)

Aristotle has no objection to the exercise of mathematics on extended bodies *in thought*. What he finds intolerable is the application of mathematics—geometry in this case—to nature, or *physis*. Geometrical space is undifferentiated space, which means that it has no "above" and "below" in itself. As I have argued, Aristotle regards "above" and "below" as irreducible characteristics of concrete space, because "above" and "below" influence the movement of natural bodies. By failing to admit these powers of *topos*, geometry obfuscates the distinguishing feature of concrete space (King 1950, 78; Duhem 1976b, 27–28).

Aristotle alerts us to another difficulty with the application of geometry to the study of bodies that come to be by *physis*. Geometry leaves open the possibility of a void (*kenon*), or what he calls "place [*topos*] bereft of body" (208b26). He understands void as completely empty, and this means it is devoid of any particularities such as the positions of "above" and "below." Thus, void is unable to account for locomotion (*phoran*) (*Physics* 4.8). In stark contrast to the mathematician, then, Aristotle wants to elaborate a concept of concrete place or *topos*, which applies to bodies as they are found in the world.[3]

While she does not say so explicitly, I believe one of the reasons Irigaray is drawn to Aristotle's classic account of *topos* is that he refuses to put perceptible bodies into the grid of abstract space. Her figuration of "place, interval," like Aristotle's *topos*, exceeds geometrical determination (IR, 167–68; E, 15–16). Bergson shares Aristotle and Irigaray's aversion to the use of geometrical space to study the relationship between bodies in nature. Bergson's conception of concrete extensity, like Aristotle's *topos* and Irigaray's "place, interval," cannot be reduced to the homogeneous space of Euclidean geometry.[4]

(MAN'S) FIRST *TOPOS*

Aristotle pursues the problem of defining *topos* by concentrating on the relationships between readily observable bodies in their immediate environs. This brings me to another important contrast between abstract space and *topos*. Where space can be conceived as embracing the whole universe, *topos* applies to the relation between a particular body and what immediately surrounds (*periechei*) it.[5] Aristotle does not deny that place can be understood as an all-embracing container of things. It can be conceived as the common place in which all bodies are (*topos o men koinos*) (209a32). But *topos* in this sense is secondary to his conception of it. Above all else, he thinks *topos* as "the special place which is the first in which a body is" (*apanta ta sōmata estin, o d' idios, en o prōto*) (209a32–33). To support his contention, he gives the following example:

> I mean . . . that you are now in the heavens because you are in the air and that is in the heavens, and you are in the air because you are in the earth and similarly in that because you are in this place which surrounds (*periechei*) nothing more than you (*su*). (*Physics* 4.209a33–209b1)

Thus, Aristotle does allow for the idea of a common place ("you" are in the heavens). But as St Thomas Aquinas has argued, "you" (*su*) are only in the common place because "you" are first of all in the special place that surrounds only "you." As St Thomas points out, the common place that "you" are in is posterior and accidental to *topos* in the proper sense, which is the first place in which a body *is* (St Thomas, 1963: 423, 195).

The status of the word "first" (*prōtē*) is ambiguous in this passage. Aristotle uses "first" in both temporal and spatial terms throughout his *oeuvre*. In temporal terms, he describes substance (*ousia*), the preeminent category, as being first of all. As we know, this means substance precedes all of the other categories of being. In contrast, according to the reading offered by St Thomas, the use of "first" in this famous example from *Physics* 4 is primarily spatial. "First" suggests an immediate relation of situation between a body and its *topos*. Yet "first place" must also be understood in temporal terms. The immediate place surrounding only "you" is thought as present, as a description of "your" current situation in a specific *topos*.

I think the temporal status of "first place" exceeds the strictures of the present moment. This overflow emerges when we acknowledge that "first place" is entwined obliquely in the relation between woman and man. In order to understand the way "first place" exceeds the "now," consider the sexuate stakes of Irigaray's reading of Aristotle in "Place, Interval."

We know that his book on *topos* is not restricted to a description of the places of human bodies; *topos* applies to all perceptible bodies (208b27–29). Nonetheless, by using a human body as the model for his argument here, Aristotle attributes a certain privilege to the place of a human being in the world. In Irigarayan terms, the scenario that he describes is not sexually neutral. The addressee of his text–"you" (*su*)– is male, while the first *topos* that surrounds (*periechei*) nothing more than "you" is woman's body (ESD, 35–36; E, 41–42).[6]

By itself, the pronoun "you" (*su*) does not have masculine connotations. The Greek *su*, like the English "you," is unmarked by gender. It is not enough to fall back on the justification that Aristotle's lectures were delivered to male students in order to argue for the masculinity of "you."[7] The masculine sexuation of the body described in this passage is established through the *relation* between "you" and the first (*prōtē*) container surrounding (*periechein*) "you." In broad terms, Irigaray contends that the very concept of a container—which bears upon conceptuality as such—is bound up with woman's body, while the concept of a thing or a human body is bound up with man and the male embryo.

How does Irigaray's sexuate engagement with *Physics* 4 bring out a reading of "first place" that exceeds the apparent presentism of Aristotle's figuration? Her text suggests that "first place" is legible as a symptom of man's nostalgic longing for a return to his first place, the mother's womb. In this sense, the concept of *topos* is an expression of desire for an impossibly lost and irretrievable present.

While Irigaray's reading of Aristotle complicates his presentist account of *topos* as the first place of a body by rendering the spectre of the mother explicit in his discourse, she does not affirm this nostalgic figuration of temporality. On the contrary, Irigaray's "Place, Interval" and the introduction to *An Ethics of Sexual Difference* call for a rethinking of time beyond (the desire for) presence. She wants to think time as an open threshold to the past and the future, which exceeds all attempts at containment. Irigaray's engagement with temporality implies spatiality as well. In short, place in her work must be understood in both of these senses; it designates an enduring and extensive relation between bodies.

The next section discusses Aristotle's use of an analogy between place and a vessel to develop his concept of *topos*. This analogy is important to my argument for several reasons. In ancient Greek thinking (and in Western thought more generally) the figure of the vessel (*angeion*) is bound up with woman's body.[8] For Irigaray, the fact that Aristotle appeals to an analogy between place and vessel is one of the traces that betray the way in which the concept of *topos* is entangled with the status of sexual difference. Given the extreme complexity of Aristotle's account of place, I will postpone detailed discussion of Irigaray's reading of *topos* and vessel as woman until Chapter Three.

"AS WINE IS IN A JAR, A BODY IS IN PLACE"

To deduce his concept of *topos*, Aristotle introduces an analogy. He suggests that place is something like a vessel (*angeion*) (208b2–3; 210a24). This analogy between vessel and *topos* allows Aristotle to demonstrate that place is not to be confused with the body it contains. In his terms, a thing has a *topos* when the thing is said to "be in something else" (*estai en allōi*) (210a25). Being *en topōi* is not the only way a body is in another thing; it is, nonetheless, the "most basic" (*kuriōtaton*) way of being in something else, a privilege with extraordinary implications for his ontology (210a24).

To clarify the sense in which one thing is said to be in another, Aristotle sets out to establish whether or not a body can "be in itself" (*estai en autōi*). This is where the analogy between vessel and *topos* is pertinent. It gives him a way of arguing that a body is in itself only when it is contained by something else (210a25–34). He asks us to conceive of a thing in place in the same way that we think of wine (*oinos*) in a jar (*amphoreus*). When the wine and the jar are together (*hama*), they are parts (*meros*) of a whole (*holos*), and, as parts that make up a whole, they are said to be in itself. He emphasizes that these parts are different in being (*heteron to einai*) because the definition (*logos*) of "that in which" (*en ps*) is different (*allos*) from the definition of "that which is in" (*en toutōi*) it. On the basis of this analogy, he argues that a body is not in itself primarily. Nonetheless, when a body is *en topōi*, like wine in a jar, it is part of a whole, and together body and place are "in itself" (210b2–22).

Aristotle is careful to distinguish between his analogy for *topos*—the wine and the vessel—and something *en topōi* in the strict sense. For him, a vessel is like a place, except that a vessel can be moved around. *Topos*, on the other hand, is a nonportable vessel (209b28–29). In spite of this contrast, the analogy between vessel and place is crucial to his argument. It reveals an important requirement for the concept of *topos*. Like a vessel containing wine, a place surrounding a body is not part of that body. Body and place are in a contiguous rather than a continuous relationship.

The analogy between vessel and place gives Aristotle a way to exclude three plausible candidates for *topos*: form (*morphē, eidos*), matter (*hylē*), and an interval (*diastēma*) in corporeal body. It also enables his definition of *topos* as the first immobile limit surrounding a body (*periechontos peras akinēton prōton*). To assert that Aristotle's analogy enables his definition of place is to suggest that the separation he maintains between vessel and *topos* is less stable than he admits. On the one hand, he takes pains to distinguish his analogy of a vessel containing liquid from a body in place in the strict sense. On the other hand, I argue that the very definition of *topos* is bound up with the definition of the vessel.

DEFINING *TOPOS* THROUGH THE "ANALOGY" OF THE VESSEL

Aristotle believes there are four plausible alternatives for the concept of place: form, matter, interval, and the first immobile limit surrounding a body. Because *topos* is the first thing surrounding a body, form (*morphē, eidos*) could appear to be place, because form, like *topos*, functions as a kind of limit (*peras*) that bounds a body. But the form of a body is different from its *topos*. Form is inseparable from the body; it functions as a limit that gives a thing its shape (*morphē*) and definition. Place, as we know from the analogy between *topos* and vessel, is separable (*chōristos*). For Aristotle, it is the very separability of *topos* and the body it surrounds (*periechei*) that alerts the natural scientist to the existence of place (209b1–7; 209b23–31; 211b10–13).

We know from Chapter One that matter (*hylē*) is a characterless substratum. It has the capacity to be white when it was previously black and to be hard when it used to be soft. According to Aristotle, it is from this perspective that some people think that matter is *topos*; they believe these changes in the form abiding with the substratum of a thing are of the same kind as a change "where air was but now there is water." For Aristotle, however, these alterations are irreducible. When something becomes white that used to be black, it has been changed by form, and this kind of alteration in matter is inseparable from that body. In contrast, place is what holds a body. So, when water comes to occupy a *topos* where air used to be, it is not the place that has been changed by form but the contents of *topos* that have altered. Place is separable from the thing it surrounds, while matter cannot be separated from the thing (211b29–212a1). That matter is devoid of specificity also means that it can have no shape (*morphē*) of its own. Place, on the other hand, is necessarily characterized by the capacity to surround a body (209b23–31).

The third candidate for the concept of *topos* that Aristotle confronts is an interval (*diastēma*) between the extremities of place and the body it surrounds (211b14–19). Before exploring his treatment of this concept in relation to *topos*, the meanings of the word *diastēma* deserve our attention. *Diastēma* is central to Irigaray's transvaluation of Aristotle and to my own concerns in this book. In ancient Greek, *diastēma*, like the English "interval," has both spatial and temporal connotations. For instance, Aristotle uses *diastēma* to describe the radius of a sphere and a ratio (212a18). In Plato's *Republic*, *diastēma* is the name for the intervals between notes in music (1970, 531a4).[9] *Diastēma* is also used in Aristotelian logic to refer to the relation between terms in a syllogism (42b10, 82b7). According to Liddell and Scott, *diastēma* also means "difference" and "sublimity."[10]

In Aristotle's discourse on *topos*, the *diastēma*, if it exists, would be a kind of empty space or void (*kenon*) between the limits of the containing body (or vessel, in the terms of his analogy) and the thing it surrounds. The *diastēma* is conceived primarily in spatial terms here, although, of course, its very presence between the limits of a vessel and the body it contains is temporal as well.

According to Aristotle, the phenomenon of mutual replacement (*antiperistasis*) suggests that *topos* is a corporeal interval. Like a vessel, a place is immobile, while the thing it contains often moves about, as, for example, when water leaves a vessel to be replaced by air. What is in between (*metaxu*) the water and the air is thought to be something over and above the water changing position (211b14–17). But Aristotle refutes the thesis of the *diastēma* vehemently. If a corporeal interval did exist, there would be an infinite number of places in the same spot. Both the water and air would be surrounded by intervals, and all of the parts of the water and all of the parts of the air would also be surrounded by intervals. This means there would be an infinite number of intervals overlapping each other (21b20–24). For Aristotle, this is impossible. The parts of each body are in continuous relation with the other parts of that body, which means there can be no intervals within the body of water or within the body of air. And when water flows out of a vessel, the air with which the water is contiguous rushes in to replace it. There is thus no *diastēma* between the two bodies changing place, the water and the air touch one another directly (211b17–20).

There is another consequence of affirming the interval as place that Aristotle cannot tolerate. Mutual replacement involves the movement of the two bodies exchanging positions. This means that the intervals around each body (and, indeed, the infinite number of intervals surrounding all of the parts that make up each body) must move (211b21–24). In other words, if *topos* is a *diastēma*, it must be mobile. But he is convinced that place is motionless; otherwise, he cannot explain locomotion, the distinguishing feature of *topos* (211a12–13). The reason a mobile concept of place is unacceptable to him is that locomotion is defined as change of place, and this definition is predicated on the assumption that *topos* does not move (208a31).

Aristotle's rendering of the interval here elides its fundamental importance to the concept of place. His dismissal of the *diastēma* is based on a compartmentalized understanding of the "concept" of the interval in terms of presence. He construes the *diastēma* as an empty space that *is* between bodies. For Irigaray, the interval must be thought of as extensive and embodied. And in stark contrast to Aristotle, she does not believe that the temporality of the interval is something that can be presented as such; the interval, inextricably bound up with place and body, is the very threshold from which place and duration emerge. In this sense, Irigaray's interval cannot be present to thought, because the interval seeps beyond the present to the past and to the future. As a temporal relation that overflows specification in terms of the present, the interval is excessive and cannot be enclosed in a definition. In his preoccupation with conceiving of *topos* in terms of presence, Aristotle does not cognize the irreducibility of the interval to the thinking of place.

While Aristotle's concept of place implies temporality, his explicit construal of *topos* is confined to thinking the *present* relation between a body and its place. This pronounced tendency in his argument leads him to discount the possibility of thinking *topos* as a *diastēma* or interval. I suggested earlier that Irigaray discerns a time of longing by man for his mother and that this time is implicitly at work in the relation between place and the body it circumscribes. This nostalgic order of temporality opens a chasm in the present relation between thing and *topos* to a past that is neither wholly absent (otherwise the maternal container would not be cognizable) nor wholly present. Here, time is no longer harnessed to the calculable time that authorizes Aristotle's refutation of the interval.

Once he rejects matter, form, and an interval in corporeal body as candidates for the concept of place, he is able to define *topos*. Once again, the analogy between vessel and place is central to his discussion. He writes:

> Just as the vessel is place which can be carried around [*metaphoritos*], so place is a vessel which cannot be moved around [*ametakinēton*]. So when something moves inside something which is moving and the thing inside moves about (e.g. a boat on a river), the surrounding thing functions for it as a vessel rather than as a place; place is meant to be unchangeable [*akinētos*], so that it is the whole river, rather, that is the place, because as a whole it is unchangeable [*akinētos*]. (So that is what place is: the first unchangeable limit of that which surrounds) [*hōste to tou periechontos peras akinēton prōtōn, tout estin o topos*]. (*Physics* 4.212a14–21)

This difficult passage has generated much controversy. The problem turns on his insistence that *topos* is unchangeable or motionless (*akinētos*). Aristotle does explain the situation of the boat without violating the principle of immobility. He proposes that the first limit of the boat—the water flowing around it—functions not as a place but rather as a vessel, but this still fails to explain the *topos* of the boat. What is the place of the boat? For Bergson, Alexander of Aphrodisias, Simplicius, and Duhem, the place of the boat must be the riverbanks, because the banks of the river are the first unchangeable limit (*peras akinēton prōtōn*) of the boat (Bergson 1970, 50–1; 65–66).[11] Yet as King points out, this plainly contradicts one of Aristotle's specific requirements for the concept of *topos*, which is that place should be neither greater (*elatto*) nor lesser (*meizo*) than the thing it surrounds (King 1950, 89; 211a1–2). Here we find a striking incompatibility between Aristotle's specification that *topos* must be motionless and his requirement that place is no greater or lesser than the body it holds *en topōi* (Ross in Aristotle 1936, 57–58; King, 88–91).

I think Aristotle's commitment to the immobility of *topos* must be privileged over his requirement that place is no greater or lesser than what it contains, because motionlessness is explicitly specified in his definition (212a20–21). And the consequences of identifying *topos* with the immediate limits of the flowing river would be disastrous for his argument. It would mean that the distinction between place and vessel must be collapsed, a distinction that he takes great pains to maintain in *Physics* 4. Therefore, I concur with Bergson, Alexander, Simplicius, and Duhem: the place of the boat in Aristotle's argument is the riverbanks, which are immobile.

That is not to say I agree with him. There are tremendous problems with insisting on the immobility of place. Aristotle's concept of *topos* fails as soon as we acknowledge that a containing body can be moved (King 1950, 91; Ross in Aristotle 1936, 56–58; Casey 1998, 70; Hussey 1983, xxx–xxxi). While he gets around this problem, of moving bodies containing a thing, by arguing that a mobile containing body functions as a vessel rather than a place, the reader is left wondering how useful his theory of place is, given that all bodies have the capacity to move?

In the very passage where he defines *topos*, Aristotle grants the vessel status as a concept in its own right. Where place surrounds an immobile being, the vessel circumscribes mobile bodies, such as a boat moving in a river. Given that all bodies have a capacity for motion, it seems to me that in the Aristotelian universe the vessel has a wider application than does place. In short, by virtue of its mobility, the concept of the vessel threatens to overtake the concept of *topos* in the strict sense.

It is valuable to recall some of the central features of Aristotle's difficult conceptualization of *topos* in *Physics* 4. When a thing is in place, it is surrounded by another body, which is different in being from the thing it circumscribes. Being *en topōi* thus designates a contiguous relation of situation between an immobile container and a contained body.[12]

While *topos* is a relational concept, Aristotle does not address the very status of the *relation between* the containing body and the thing it circumscribes. By defining place as "the first unchangeable limit of that which surrounds," he focuses on the limit of one body rather than engaging with the difference between "that which surrounds" and the body in place (212a21). In stark contrast, Irigaray is specifically concerned with this differential threshold. This threshold—the Irigarayan interval—is not something that can be presented to thought, because this "concept" is an opening to the past and to the future. The temporal undecidability of Irigaray's interval renders the supposed presence of the two bodies implied in Aristotle's concept of *topos* (what surrounds and what is surrounded) far more complex than he acknowledges. We will return to this question in the next chapter.

We know that Aristotle restricts the applicability of *topos* to perceptible bodies, yet I suggested in the introduction that substance, his highest concept, is obliquely dependent on place.

BEING IN PLACE

Aristotle denies univocity to being. The highest general concepts in his ontology are the categories substance (*ousia*), quantity (*poson*), quality (*poion*), relation (*pros ti*), place (*topos*), time (*chronos*), a posture (*keishtai*), a having (*echein*), a doing (*poien*), and a being affected (*paschein*). One of the categories is explicitly privileged over the others, substance (*ousia*). For Aristotle, "substance is primary in every sense—in formula [*kai logōi*], in knowledge [*kai gnōsei*], in time [*kai chronōi*]. For of the other categories none can exist independently, but only substance" (*Metaphysics* 1028a31–35). Place is manifestly subordinate to *ousia*.

Yet in a crucial passage in *Physics* 4, being *en topōi* is presented as the condition of possibility for securing the identity of his primary category (210a15–24). This is not a maneuver Aristotle assimilates. It is an eruption in his corpus where place overflows its dependence on substance to serve, paradoxically, as its enabling ground.

Before turning to this extraordinary passage in the *Physics*, I want to emphasize the divergence between Aristotle's category of substance and his concept of place. As Chapter One explained, *ousia* is the species-form (*eidos*). In the *Metaphysics*, *ousia* is defined as "one":

> All the attributes in the definition [*horismos*] *must* be one [*en to*]; for the definition is a single formula [*logos*] and a formula of substance [*ousia*], so that it must be a formula of some one thing [*autōn einai logon*]; for substance means a "one" [*hen ti*] and "this" [*tode ti*]. (*Physics* 4.1037b25–28)

This preeminent category does not consist of independent elements; it is defined as one in being (*autōn einai logon*): For instance, Socrates and Callias are materially different, but as human beings both are "the same in form, for their form is indivisible [*tauto de tōi eidei atomon gar to eidos*]" (1034a5–9). In contrast, when a body is *en topōi*, that body is said to be in something else (*allo en allōi*) (*Physics* 210a25). Aristotle does tell us that a thing in place constitutes a whole (*holon*), but this whole is not defined as one in being (*autōn einai logon*) in the sense that substance is, for place consists of a relation between two things that are different in being (*heteron to einai*): a contained body and the first unchangeable limit of what surrounds (*periechontos peras akinēton prōtōn*) (210b16, 212a20–21).

We saw earlier that Aristotle does not believe that place is reducible to the matter of a perceptible body. It is, nonetheless, a concept that is restricted to beings that have matter; *topos* is a relation between sensible bodies. This means it is finite. For instance, a place is destroyed when the surrounding body of which the unchangeable limits of *topos* are made pass out of existence (210a10). But the destruction of a sensible body does not impact on the being of substance. It is completely independent of the material substratum even though it serves as the very source (*archē*) of things that come to be by *physis* and *technē*.

In short, *ousia*, unlike *topos*, is eternal (1033b5–7; Lear 1988, 280). Finally, *topos* is a relation of situation between perceptible bodies, and perceptible bodies are ultimately dependent on *eidos*, their very *ousia*, to have being. This would seem to render the primacy of substance irrefutable.

In the opening paragraph of the third chapter of *Physics* 4, Aristotle radically undermines the primacy of substance as an uncreated and independent unity by positing being-in-place as the most basic (*kuriōtaton*) way in which "one thing is said to be in another" (*allo en allōi*). He writes:

> Next we must find in how many ways one thing is said to be *in* another. (1) In one way, as the finger is in [*en ti*] the hand, and generally, the part in [*en*] the whole. (2) In another, as the whole is in [*en*] the parts—the whole does not exist apart from the parts. (3) In another, as man is in [*en*] animals and, generally, form is in genus [*eidos en genēi*]. (4) In another, as the genus is in the form, and, generally, the part of the form in the definition [*eidos en tos logos*]. (5) In another, as health is in hot and cold things, and generally, as the form is in the matter [*eidos en te hylē*]. (6) In another, as the affairs of Greece are in [the hands of] the king [of Persia], and, generally, as [things are] in the first thing productive of change [*proto kinētiko*]. (7) In another, as [a thing is] in its good, and, generally, in its end, (that is, the that-for-for-the-sake-of-which [*ti esti*]). (8) And (the most basic way of all) as [a thing is] in a vessel and generally, in a place [*pantin de kuriōtaton to os en angeiōi kai olos en topos*]. (*Physics* 4.210a15–24)

Being in place, the last modality presented in this list, is the most basic (*kuriōtaton*) way of being in something else (*allo en allōi*). The surprise for readers familiar with Aristotle's doctrine on the primacy of substance emerges when he lists the third and fourth senses of being in. Both of these ways of being in explicitly include concepts that are essential to the doctrine of substance: the being of substantial form in the genus (*eidos en genēi*) and the being of the form (*eidos*) in the definition or formula (*logos*) of substance. This is perhaps most striking in his presentation of the fourth way of being in, "as the genus is in the form, and, generally, the part of the form is in the definition [*eidos en tos logos*]" (210a17–20). Do we not have a contradiction between asserting that *ousia* is primary in every sense—in formula (*logos*), in knowledge, in time—and the stipulation in this passage from the *Physics* that being *en topōi* is the most basic (*kuriōtaton*) way in which a thing is said to be in something else (1028a31–32, 210a24)?

A reader striving to remain faithful to the priority of *ousia* might try to get around the troubling attribution of "most basic" status to place by arguing that the ways in which *eidos* is in its genus and that *eidos en tos logos* are to be understood metaphorically. Here metaphor would be deployed in traditionally Aristotelian terms as secondary to the privileged form of philosophical discourse, definition (97b31–39, 139b32–140a1). For me, the gesture of subordinating the ideal attributes that make *ousia* one in being to a material relation designated by the concept of *topos* and a body enveloped by place is suggestive of the possibility of a different thinking where the sensible is not subordinate or separable from ideality.

In order to understand the complicated relationship between *ousia* and a body *en topōi*, one of the central phrases of this passage demands some clarification, the phrase "a thing being in another" (*allo en allōi*) (210a15). The word *en* is not strictly reducible to the English preposition "in." It can also be translated as "on," "within," and "at." *En* shares with these English prepositions temporal and spatial meanings. For instance, to be "*en Athinisi*" is to be in Athens both in the sense of being in place and in the sense of being there at the present time (Hussey in Aristotle 1983b, 107–8).[13]

The status of *allo* in the phrase "*allo en allō*" also needs elaboration. *Allo*, which Hussey translates as "thing," is frequently rendered in English as "other" or "different." *Allōi* is the dative form of *allo*. In short, these words *allo* and *allōi* refer to beings that are different from one another. What kind of difference in being? Aristotle insists that being (*to on*) is said in many ways (*legetai pollachōs*), and the categories denote the several senses in which being is said (Brentano 1975, 58). For Aristotle, *allo* is a derivative of being (*to on*), which means it must have a specific meaning in relation to each category (1018a35).[14] Given that *ousia* is being (*to on*) in the primary sense, the phrase *allo en allōi* necessarily implies a relation between substantial beings.[15]

What does it mean when Aristotle declares that the most basic (*kuriōtaton*) way of *allo en allōi* is to be *en topōi* (210a24)? I have argued that, when a body is *en topōi*, it dwells in something that is irreducibly other in being. The concept of *topos* is founded on difference. Without doubt, difference is thought here in terms of the difference between two bodies that are present to each other. There is no direct reference in Aristotle's discourse to a temporal difference that exceeds presentation in terms of a current relation between two bodies. This presentist figuration of difference between a body and its place is significant, though, because he affirms that it is the "most basic" way of being in something else (*allo en allōi*).

Two of the subordinate ways of *allo en allōi* in the list involve the definition of substance, the being of (3) *eidos en genēi* and (4) *eidos en tos logos*. In the *Metaphysics* the being of the form in the genus and of the form in the *logos* is defined as one in being (1037b25–28). But in this strange passage from *Physics* 4, the ideality and oneness of *ousia* are dependent on the sensible relation between a body and its place (210a15–24).

I am not suggesting that Aristotle explicitly affirms that *topos* grounds his highest category. Why? Because place is the limit of a perceptible body, and all perceptible bodies have their source (*archē*) in *eidos*, which is the *ousia* of things. That is to say, *topos* cannot be thought without the being of *eidos*. Yet, at the same time, *Physics* 4 betrays difference and the sensible at heart of the "oneness" and ideality of *ousia*. We have arrived at a stammering in Aristotle's thought.

THE SENSIBLE RELATION

Chapter One suggested that the figuration of difference in Aristotle is highly ambivalent. On the one hand, difference is subordinated to securing the identity of the categories in the *Metaphysics* (1054b23–26; 1055a5–15). On the other hand, there are a couple of oscillations in the same treatise where the being of difference is affirmed beyond the identity of the genera (998b22–23; 1018a12–14). But the moments where difference erupts in his discourse are fleeting. Aristotle is overwhelmingly inclined to efface difference and to privilege the identity of the categories.

In "How to Conceive (of) a Girl?" Irigaray reads Aristotle's tendency to efface difference as an expression of phallomorphism. For instance, he elevates the explicitly masculine concept of species-form (*eidos*) as the very substance (*ousia*) of things that come to be by *physis* (193a35–b4). In contrast, the female sex, menstrual fluid, and matter are denigrated in his oeuvre (728a26–30, 726a34b1, 737a27–29, 192a14–23). For Irigaray, these derogatory assessments betray an anxiety in Aristotle. Perhaps the source (*archē*) of *physis* is not form (*eidos*) but the mother (Irigaray S, 161/SA, 201)?

On careful inspection, Irigaray finds that Aristotle's figuration of the female sex is contradictory. He consistently debases her, and yet woman also overflows her role to confound herself with matter *and* privation. Paradoxically, according to Irigaray, woman-matter is both being *and* not-being (S, 165/SA, 206). I argued that the ontological uncontainability of woman-matter is a trace of both the maternal-feminine and the interval of sexual difference. In this context, the interval elevates Aristotle's conceptual architecture as phallocentrism and situates the maternal-feminine as the disavowed ground of philosophy. In short, the interval institutes philosophy as a sexed hierarchy. Woman-matter, then, is a tremendously threatening figure in Aristotelian metaphysics because she has the potential to betray the violent obfuscation on which his thought is predicated.

This chapter has suggested that Aristotle's concept of *ousia*, which is posited as primary in every sense, is obscurely dependent on the relational concept of *topos*. Yet place in Aristotle also depends on substance. *Topos* is the first immobile limit of that which surrounds, and the *archē* of the surrounding body is *ousia*. What is the significance of this contradictory entanglement? The identity of Aristotelian substance is fractured by the relational concept of place. This suggests that thinking does not begin with the concept of substance outside time and place; on the contrary, thinking emerges as and through a sensible relation. Perhaps the emergence of this sensible relation should no longer be conceived on the basis of the identity of two substantial beings in contiguity with one another? And perhaps the relation is the very condition on which being is articulated?

I have argued that the presentist figuration of being *en topōi* in Aristotle traces the limit of the surrounding body rather than what lies *between* the containing body and the thing in place. In order to think the sensible relation of *topos* and body as the opening of thinking, it is no longer possible to conceive of place in terms of a present relation between a body and its *topos*. Irigaray's sexuate reading of Aristotle is particularly concerned with overcoming the presentist orientation of his formulation in order to allow place to be posited as the opening to the past and to the future. This opening is the interval of sexual difference.

3. The Aporia between Envelope and Things

The relationship between envelope and things
constitutes one of the aporias, or the aporia, of Aristotelianism
and of the philosophical systems derived from it.

IRIGARAY ESD, 10/E, 17

The only difference between the love which flows through
the envelope-walls of our skin or mucous fluids and the love
which appropriates for itself in and by the same,
lies in the 'through' which allows each one
their living becoming.

IRIGARAY 1992, 27/1982, 32

IRIGARAY'S INTRODUCTION to *An Ethics of Sexual Difference* and the essay "Place, Interval" are among the most important texts in the evolution of her thinking. In these works, she goes beyond a critical description of the constitutive phallocentrism of metaphysics to articulate a nonhierarchical figuration of sexual difference.[1] Significantly, for my purposes, her formulation of sexual difference is developed in relation to Aristotle. I argue in this chapter that the interval—difference, the threshold from which the sexes are generated—is in some ways a tribute to his thinking on place (ESD, 40/E, 46).

Irigaray's nonhierarchical formulation of sexual difference builds on her critical description of Aristotle in "How to Conceive of (a) Girl?" In the introduction to *An Ethics of Sexual Difference* and in "Place, Interval," she reaffirms the maternal-feminine as the disavowed outside of his project, an outside that functions as the secret foundation of philosophy (IR, 169; ESD, 10 34–6/E, 18, 41–2). What is new in these works is the emphasis she confers on the interval. Irigaray acknowledges the interval in "How to Conceive (of) a Girl?" as well. In this early text, she demonstrates that the interval is tangled up with the maternal-feminine. Together these amorphic figures are excluded from the phallomorphic metaphysics of Aristotle, although their exclusion is not entirely successful. Traces of the maternal-feminine and the interval are legible in his corpus in the formulation of the evil of the infinite (S, 167/SA, 208).

In the introduction to *An Ethics of Sexual Difference* and in "Place, Interval," Irigaray sets out to dissociate the interval from the maternal-feminine and to consider the interval as the generative relation between the sexes. This gesture also allows her to overcome the acute sexual violence of Aristotle's conception of hylomorphism. By foregrounding the interval as the threshold of becoming between matter and form, she is able to rethink these concepts nonhierarchically. While Irigaray refuses the hierarchical sexuation of Aristotle's theory of matter and form, she affirms these concepts as sexed in order to revalue sexual difference. And yet, because she engages in this revaluation through a thought of the interval, which is necessarily open, she also maintains the possibility of reconceiving matter and form in terms that are not primarily sexed (ESD, 49/E, 54).

I have suggested that the interval is inspired by Aristotle's conception of *topos*. This maneuver would be puzzling if we read place, as it usually is in Aristotelian scholarship, as a subordinate category to the highest concept of being, first substance (*prōto ousia*) (1026a18–22, 1061b1–17). But Irigaray does not construe place in subordination to the highest concept in Aristotle. On the contrary, she contends that the relation between a body and its place is fundamental to his project and the Western tradition (IR, 169/ESD, 10/E, 17). Let us go into this in more detail.

In the introduction to *An Ethics of Sexual Difference*, Irigaray makes an aphoristic claim that is central to her argument in "Place, Interval." She writes, "The relationship [*rapport*] between envelope and things constitutes one of the aporias, or the aporia, of Aristotelianism and of the philosophical systems derived from it" (IR, 169/ESD, 10/E, 17).[2] Aristotle regards an aporia as a puzzle or difficulty that arises from the struggle to reconcile two or more plausible beliefs (Urmson 1990, 30).

In this sense, an aporia is something to overcome. Irigaray's use of "aporia" must be distinguished from the Aristotelian sense of the word; for her, an aporia involves a paradoxical entanglement of concepts that overflows all attempts at resolution. This does not constitute a failure of thought, as it would for Aristotle. On the contrary, an aporia is an opening to thinking the interval of sexual difference.

We encountered a striking instance of the aporetic relation between envelope and things in Chapter Two, where I argued that the identity of substance depends paradoxically on the way in which a thing is in its place. For Irigaray the relationship between envelope and things is not sexually neutral. Man's body is entangled in Aristotle's conception of a thing, while the ambiguous sexuation of woman's body is bound up in his concept of *topos* (ESD, 10–11, 34–55/E, 17–8, 41–59). Irigaray does not endorse the analogy of woman with place and man with the body in place. She regards this figuration as phallocentric. It is through diagnosing the sexed hierarchy at work in Aristotle's construal of place and thing that Irigaray begins to articulate a way to move beyond his phallocentrism. She discerns remainders at work in the relationship between woman and man. Irigaray finds that woman-*topos* is an uncontainable volume. In other words, she asserts that Aristotle's concept of *topos* leaks, and this porous vessel spells trouble not only for the understanding of place as an immobile limit (*peras*) surrounding a body; woman-place radically undermines the identity of the concept of substance (212a20). We could say woman conceives, without, however, confining herself to the strictures of conceptuality.

To assert that Aristotle's concept of place overflows the very limits it purports to establish does not institute nonhierarchical sexual difference as the opening to thought and life. Nonetheless, this critical gesture is indispensable to Irigaray's argument. It prepares the way for the articulation of the interval as a mobile and excessive opening that engenders radical sexual difference (IR, 167–68; ESD, 7–8, 48–49/E, 15–16, 53–54).

The phallocentric nature of the relationship between a body in place and the figuration of the sexes is the focus of much of this chapter. Irigaray's discourse moves from describing the way Aristotle explicitly construes the aporia between woman-place and man-thing, to drawing out the excessive implications of this relationship. These excesses are traces of the interval that Irigaray transvalues in order to engender an opening for sexual difference. I analyze several modalities of interval—placenta, mucus, and the interval between matter and form. Strictly speaking, the interval is outside the order of number, because the interval remains open to articulations beyond being.

Irigaray's interval is sensible-transcendental. To put this in other terms, the interval is the threshold from which matter and form are reconceived. She is particularly attentive to the specific relations the interval engenders. The placenta is articulated in relation to fetus and mother, the mucus emerges in relation to woman's subjectivity and in relation to an ethics of carnality. For Irigaray, carnality is not simply the site of sexual relations. In "Place, Interval," heterosexual carnality is revalued as an important context in which sexual difference takes place. Despite her tendency to focus on heterosexuality, I argue that her work also has significant implications for theorizing the ethics of homosexual carnalities.

WOMAN: THE PLACELESS PLACE

The figuration of sexual difference that Irigaray discerns in Aristotle's treatise on *topos* is hierarchical and predicated on the disavowal of the interval. By making this scenario explicit, Irigaray begins to subvert him. If woman is place, then place cannot be immobile, meaning that she does not function as the stable limit that Aristotle has defined. Paradoxically, woman is both place and the very unraveling of place.

While Aristotle's treatise on *topos* is presented as a sexually neutral discourse that is supposed to account for the concrete relations of situation between perceptible bodies, there are at work in his argument traces of complicity between hierarchical sexual difference and place. Chapter Two has already introduced a specific instance of this, Aristotle's ambiguous use of the expression "first" (*prōto*) to designate *topos* as "the special place which is the first in which a body is" (209a32–33). I argued that the word "first" has undecidably spatial and temporal connotations that recall the mother's womb as the place of the growing male embryo. My rendering of place here is not as foreign to Aristotle's discourse as it might initially appear. In the *Generation of Animals* (726a34–b1) he describes the womb as the *topos* of the embryo, and this is the dominant sense in which woman has functioned as place, according to Irigaray. Woman-place is conceived primarily as the womb surrounding a male fetus (ESD, 41; 50/E, 47; 55).

Irigaray does not explain in "Place, Interval" why she reads the embryo as male. But her argument in "How to Conceive (of) a Girl?" demonstrates that the proper goal of procreation in Aristotle is the production of a male child. A girl is engendered only when there is insufficient vital heat in the sperm, the moving cause of human reproduction (766b15–25; Irigaray S, 209/SA, 167). There is another way of inferring that the sex of the embryo is male in Aristotle. Form is associated with man and his semen, and a thing is defined through its form (*eidos*), which is its *archē* and substance (192a16–23, 193a35–b4, 194b27, 642a17). Irigaray's reading of the fetus as male in "Place, Interval" is thus faithful to Aristotle's theory of substance and to his beliefs about the proper *telos* of human reproduction: the creation of boys.[3]

While woman-place is primarily conceived as the envelope for the embryo, she is also figured as the container for man, or, more precisely, for his penis in traditional heterosexual "penetrative" intercourse (ESD, 41/E, 47). To my knowledge, Aristotle never designates the vagina as a place. He does, however, present woman as passive in copulation (1149b32). I think her (alleged) passivity is reminiscent of *topos*. Place is not one of the four modes of causality and must be the *motionless* limit of the body it contains (209a20–23, 212a20). Are these not attributes conventionally associated with passivity?

Irigaray emphasizes that the relationship between woman's function as a dwelling for the embryo and her vagina's figuration as a place for the man's penis are not discrete. These two places are confused in Aristotle and in the systems of thought derived from his legacy. In this entanglement, the womb's status as the primary place remains. The vagina, according to Irigaray, functions less as a place than as a perforation toward the first place, the womb (ESD, 41/E, 47).

There is another sense in which woman is place, a sense that demands our attention. Indeed, it is the most important sense of place for feminist scholars interested in rethinking woman in excess of phallocentrism. Woman is place for herself. Irigaray contends, however, that this sense of place is forbidden or rendered impossible by the terms of Aristotle's argument. In his treatise, woman is place for the embryo and for the man's penis, but she has no place of her own (ESD, 35–6; 41; 51/E, 41–2; 47; 55). When Irigaray says woman is place for herself, she already is speaking in excess of Aristotle's system.

Irigaray's contention that woman has no place should be read in relation to her claim in "How to Conceive (of) a Girl?" that woman does not yet exist (S, 166/SA, 207). She is placeless, because Aristotle's conceptual architecture precludes the possibility of thinking woman as anything other than a figure of lack. At the same time, her sexual and reproductive functions furnish his system with the concept-metaphors to define place. This violent appropriation is not acknowledged, which means that the question of what kind of place woman might be or become for herself never arises in Aristotle. Woman *is* only insofar as she functions as the immobile limit for man-embryo (IR, 169/ESD, 10/E, 17).

Chapter Two suggested that the traces of the maternal body in Aristotle's description of *topos* as the first thing surrounding a being are nostalgic. They betray man's longing for the irretrievable security of the womb. The implications of this oblique desire are interesting for the status of the vagina in heterosexual coitus. When a man's penis is inside a woman's vagina, he is striving for the impossible, a return to the maternal body. His sexual relation with woman is a failure in this sense, because he cannot return to his first place. This is what Irigaray is underlining when she argues that the vagina is less a place than a perforation toward the womb. From this perspective, man's relation with woman in traditional heterosexual "penetration" is underwritten by the loss of the maternal womb. His lover's body functions for him as a memorial that recalls his first and ultimate dwelling place (IR, 170; ESD, 11, 41/E, 18, 47). Irigaray does not allude to digital "penetration." However, I think her argument is applicable to any act by man of entering woman's vagina. Is lesbian "penetration" also underwritten by this desire for regression *in utero*? If it is, this carnal relation between women is different from the heterosexual scene Irigaray describes, for both lovers contain vagina-wombs.

The specter of woman's body is also evident in Aristotle's primary analogy for place—the vessel, or *angeion*. In his treatise on *topos*, the word *angeion* designates a vessel for holding liquid or dry substances (208b2–23, 210a24). Elsewhere in his oeuvre, Aristotle deploys the word *angeion* in relation to living bodies. He uses *angeion* to describe a *vessel* or *cavity* in the body, including the *veins*, the *lungs*, and the *female breast* (521b6, 511b7, 787b3, 692a12). While he does not say this himself, *angeion* is used in Greek to describe the *afterbirth*. Liddell and Scott tell us that an *angeion* is a *vessel* that holds money in a treasury, it is also something used by a mason and can be a *bucket pail*, a *sack* of leather, a *vessel* for holding corn, wine, or bread. *Angeion* also designates a *box* for petitions. In a related sense, *angeion* is a *receptacle* or *reservoir*, such as the *bed* of the sea. *Angeion* is also a word for a coffin or a sarcophagus. In plants, *angeion* designates the capsule. In writers subsequent to Aristotle, *angeion* becomes another word for the body itself.[4]

We know that Aristotle takes pains to distinguish *angeion* and *topos*. Place is the motionless limit surrounding a body, while a vessel is a moveable *topos* (209b28–29). In his argument, place must be immobile in order to comprehend locomotion (208a31). His reasoning, however, is highly problematic. His concept of *topos* fails as soon as we acknowledge that a surrounding body can be moved (King 1950, 91; Ross in Aristotle 1936, 56–58; Casey 1998, 70; Hussey 1983, xxx–xxxi).

Irigaray's reading of *Physics* 4 is highly critical of Aristotle's commitment to the immobility of place. By reading woman as both *topos* and *angeion*, she refuses his distinction between each concept. Woman is not merely an immobile limit of man-embryo; her sex organs dilate and contract and she does not function as a hermetic container. Her vagina emits menstrual blood and mucus, and, in negotiation with the fetus, her body propels the violent contractions of birth. As an animate being, she is much more than a mere limit to the man-embryo. Woman is mobile (ESD, 51–2/E, 55–57).

Irigaray's claim that the masculine is attracted to woman-place can be read in two senses (ESD, 39/E, 45).[5] According to the protocols of Aristotle's argument, woman is his immobile limit. His attraction to her is a manifestation of his desire to be safely enveloped by place. Yet woman exceeds her assigned role; she is a moving animate being, and the vessels her body contains are mobile and porous. In this sense, man's attraction to woman impels him toward the oblivion of place. For Irigaray, woman's excessiveness is a trace of the interval, which is the passage to the amorphic outside of his system, to the maternal-feminine (ESD, 49/ E 54).

Aristotle cannot acknowledge the abyssal implications of woman-place within his thinking. After all, man-embryo needs woman to be an immobile place in order to give limits to him and to his things (IR, 169/ESD, 10/E, 17).

To defend this conception of place, Aristotle is obliged to separate woman's function as an envelope from everything in the female sex that exceeds containment. In this way, woman continues to serve as a place for man-embryo while the dangerous becomings of her excessive body flows are designated as placeless (*sans lieu*). This has paradoxical consequences in traditional heterosexual intercourse. Woman is construed the passive place for man's sexual pleasure, while her *jouissance* has no place (ESD, 52/E, 56–57). Aristotle's refutation of the possibility that *topos* might be an interval (*diastēma*) is dependent on this separation between woman as container for man and the placelessness of her fluid becomings (211b17–24). Irigaray disputes this violent cleavage. The excessive flows of the interval are inextricable from woman-place (ESD, 52/E, 56–57).

From this point of view, the attribution of passivity to woman in copulation can be read as a trace of phallocentric anxiety (1149b32). Irigaray suggests that woman's presumed passivity is a ruse. "Hasn't woman been imagined as passive only because man would fear to lose mastery in that particular act? Which accounts for his occasional violence?" (ESD, 44/E, 49). Man's violations and appropriations of woman-place emanate from his unconscious fear of the flowing interval, which betrays the man-embryo's dependence on the maternal-feminine.

There are also traces within contemporary phallocentric discourse of the radically excessive status of woman-place. I want to examine three instances of this: the image of woman as castrator and the English "obscenities" "cunt" and "suck." These figures of discourse attest to the confusion of the maternal and the feminine, the impossibility of maintaining a separation between the concept of *topos* and the concept of the *angeion* and of maintaining the ruse of woman's alleged passivity.

The menace of woman-place to the functioning of phallocentrism is discernible in fantasies of woman as castrator. Irigaray offers a persuasive reading of this fantasy. The terrifying threat of the castrating woman is predicated on the effacement of a wish. If man's identity is projected into his penis and his penis is "cut off" by the vagina, then the man-penis is no longer severed from the mother-lover. He has achieved the impossible and returned to the safety of the maternal envelope (IR, 169/ESD, 10/E, 17–18). On Irigaray's reading, the image of the castrating woman is a trace, within phallocentrism, of the constitutive status of the maternal-feminine. Given that woman is mobile, the distinction between vessel and place is also unraveled, and woman's alleged passivity is rendered problematic by the paradoxical idea that her vagina might dismember man *or* allow him to return to the safety of the mother's body.

Figures of the castrating woman often entwine misogyny and racism together in Aristotelian terms. For example, consider the metaphorical associations of the concept of a "black hole" in modern physics. The combination of the connotations of "black" and the abyss and "hole," a well known and offensive slang word for woman's genitals, suggest a cosmic fear of castration—in this instance the identity of the man-penis is projected into the entirety of deep space at risk of being obliterated by the immense power of a collapsed star.[6]

"Cunt" and "suck," two of the best-known "obscenities" in English, can also be read as traces of the phallocentric confusion between woman's sex and her reproductive functions. The very designation of these words as obscene is a confirmation of Irigaray's argument. To call a woman (and sometimes a man) "cunt" is to insult her (or him) in the strongest terms. A cunt is thus presented as a reviled place. Drawing on Irigaray, I read this as a negation of man's intense desire to be inside the lover-mother's cunt-womb. In other words, "cunt" betrays the tremendously threatening status of the maternal-feminine as the effaced ground of phallocentrism. This suggests that dwelling inside a cunt is by no means a straightforwardly active experience. On the contrary, the "act" of traditional heterosexual "penetration" is also a submission to envelopment within the lover-mother's body. He feels possessed by the addressee, and this renders man vulnerable.[7] On the one hand then, the idea that woman is "active" in heterosexual "penetration" is buried in Aristotle and in misogynist inscriptions of "cunt." On the other hand, Aristotle's insistence that woman is passive and the fact that "cunt" is mostly construed as an obscenity gives away man's dread of woman's activity, albeit in negation (1149b32).

The word "suck" is regarded as less obscene than "cunt"—unlike the "c" word, it can be printed in the newspaper. Is "suck" homophobic or misogynist? Does it refer to a baby suckling on the maternal breast, to the sucking mouth of a man or a woman performing fellatio, to a man's rectum dilating and contracting in anal intercourse, or does it refer to the sucking of a vagina on a woman or a man's mouth or fingers or on a man's penis? Perhaps "suck" refers to all of these acts. The word "suck" is highly ambiguous. Sucking involves movement. The "sucker" constitutes his or her mouth, vagina, or rectum as a vessel that receives and manipulates another body. In this sense, the enveloped body could be read "passive." I think "suck" calls into question the traditional opposition between passivity and activity. And yet the dominant inscriptions of "suck" are derogatory; for instance, in American slang, the "sucker" is a dupe. In Australian slang a "suck" is a subject who depends on the body of another, and to be dependent is a form of passivity.

The most dependent act of sucking described here is breastfeeding, which is necessary for the baby's survival. I think this is the primary sense from which "suck" has evolved into a term of derision. The insult "suck" is yet another trace of the failure to acknowledge the maternal-feminine, the failure that founds phallocentrism.

This section began by drawing out the phallocentric sexuation of Aristotle's theory of *topos*: woman is paradoxically place for the man-embryo while having no place of her own. I suggested that his argument strives to constrain woman-place within the strictures of immobility. Irigaray demonstrates, however, that woman-place overflows the protocols of his definition. She is mobile, she emits fluids and contains porous vessels that expand and contract. We have just seen a number of instances in Aristotle and contemporary discourse of woman's radically subversive status as both place *and* the collapse of place.

Drawing out woman-place as the figure for *topos* and as the collapse of place is not sufficient to articulate sexual difference nonhierarchically. Woman must be rethought beyond her construal as *topos* for the man-embryo. She must become a place for herself and a place for other women. And man cannot continue to derive his *topos* from the woman-envelope; he must become place for himself, for other men, and for woman. This task requires an upheaval of Aristotle's definition of *topos*. Place must be reconceived as a moving and porous threshold in specific relation to each sex. To do this, Irigaray engages in a rethinking of the interval.

BEYOND THE LIMIT(S) OF PLACE: RETHINKING THE INTERVAL

While Aristotle's concept of place designates a contiguous situation between two bodies, his definition of *topos* as the first immobile limit of the body enveloping a thing elides the possibility of thinking the very threshold between them (212a20–21). For Irigaray, this has dire consequences, for the relationship between envelope and things is precisely the aporia that calls for thinking if place and sexual difference are to be articulated. Her entire essay "Place, Interval" is directed toward foregrounding this aporia as an opening for thought. This opening is the interval, and for Irigaray the interval is nothing other than the condition of place (ESD, 48/E, 53).

Irigaray's "interval" (*l'intervalle*) is a citation of the *diastēma*, one of the candidates Aristotle considers and then rejects in his search for the concept of *topos* (ESD, 48–49/E, 53–54). He suggests that the *diastēma* emerges as a candidate for *topos* in the context of mutual replacement. For example, when water departs from a vessel to be replaced by air, a *diastēma* would be a gap surrounding the water. This interval is regarded as independent of the air that takes the place of the departing water. That is not all. The air that comes in to replace the water would also be bounded by a *diastēma*, and all of the parts of the water and all of the parts of the air would have intervals (211b14–17).

Aristotle refutes this scenario on two counts. First, if place is an interval and intervals bound both the water and the air and all of the parts of each of these bodies, there would be an infinite number of places in the same spot. This is intolerably paradoxical. For Aristotle, a *topos* does not contain more than one body at a time. Second, given that mutual replacement involves the movement of both bodies, the intervals around the water and the air (and the infinite number of intervals bounding the parts of each body) would also be mobile. This is impossible because it would violate his commitment to the motionlessness of *topos* (211b17–24, 212b25).

The very reasons Aristotle provides for rejecting the *diastēma* compel Irigaray toward affirming the interval as place (ESD, 48/E, 53). For her, place must be mobile and must embrace an incalculable "number" of places, at least virtually. That is not to say that her conception of the interval is reducible to the *diastēma*, for she does not believe that the interval is an empty space or void that is between bodies. The construal of the interval as a void is a direct consequence of Aristotle's presentism. Because he can conceive of *topos* (and all of the categories of being) only as present, he is unable to acknowledge that the interval might exist in excess of any determination in the present. But this is precisely how Irigaray's interval must be understood. She writes that "the interval always remains in play as place, or as the possibility of place" (*l'intervalle reste toujours en jeu comme lieu, ou la possibilité du lieu*) (translation modified; ESD, 49/E, 54). For Irigaray, the interval cannot be presented as a concept, and place is never given or determined. *The interval always remains in play*. In this sense, the incalculable "number" of places implied by the interval is temporal.

To emphasize the temporality of the interval does not amount to a denial of the interval's materiality. The interval is incarnated through sensible phenomena, and in Irigaray's work these incarnations emerge through the living bodies of women and men. These sensible incarnations are thresholds to the past and to the future. This does not mean that the interval manifests these other times; rather, the interval is a threshold that gestures toward the impossibility of mastering place and time. Why? The past inscribed through and as place remains beyond recuperation in the present, and the futures inscribed as place cannot be anticipated by definition. In order to flesh out Irigaray's argument, let me return to her reading of Aristotle.

Woman's excessiveness is catastrophic for his theory of the physical world, but the consequences for woman are even worse. The flesh of her body, the vessels she contains within herself, her relations with her body fluids, with plants, with animals, with man, with another woman, with a fetus during pregnancy, and with other aspects of her milieu are illegible. She has no limit to distinguish herself from other bodies in the world, so in Aristotle's account of *topos* there is never any idea that woman's skin might be the envelope limiting her bodily identity. The "envelope" of the skin Irigaray describes here is a threshold of the interval (ESD, 50/E, 55).

For Irigaray, the interval is the stake (*enjeu*) of desire, the cause of man-embryo's locomotion toward woman-place. In the wake of her radical formulation of the interval, she contends that Aristotle's fixation on conceiving woman-*topos* as an immobile limit should be read as an (impossible) desire to surmount the interval. Within the terms of his model of *topos*, the passage toward place is a doomed attempt at intrauterine regression. The interval is devoured on this model, and this leads to a destruction of the alterity of woman-place. She cannot be place for herself because she is consumed in her function as the envelope for man-embryo (ESD, 48/E, 53).

Yet Aristotle's concept of *topos* fails. Specters of the interval seep from the ambiguous sexuation of woman-place. In his argument, these specters have no specificity; they are solidified into his conceptualization of *topos* as an immobile limit or are designated as placeless fluids (ESD, 48/E, 53). In order to transvalue his theory of *topos* and articulate sexual difference nonhierarchically, Irigaray distinguishes several modalities of interval. To be precise, the interval is not one or multiple but outside the order of number. "It" exceeds number, because the emergence of (an) interval as a threshold always overflows the present and seeps into futures that may never come into being.

"Two" of these are particular to woman's body—the membranes enveloping a fetus and the mucus (ESD, 48; 49/E, 53; 54). She also affirms the interval as the threshold between matter and form (IR, 167/ESD, 7–8/E, 15). Her articulation of the interval between matter and form is crucial for the possibility of thinking place as an interval generative of relations that do not have being. In the final section of this chapter I address her inscription of the interval in relation to matter and form; but first, I want to discuss the placenta and the mucus. These "two" figurations of the interval are related to her elaboration of woman as place in multiple senses. They also prepare the ground for a theory of place that is no longer collapsible into woman's body.

PLACENTA

For Irigaray, everything delimited by place on the Aristotelian model, whether animate or inanimate, is traced with man's nostalgic longing for his first dwelling, the womb. This is bound up in Aristotle's presentism. The presentism of his account of *topos* is evident in his inclination to discuss the place of a body not only as it is now but also as the effaced *desire* for an irretrievable present, the state of being in the maternal body. The interval is the stake (*enjeu*) of desire, which man strives to overcome. Aristotle's definition of place buries the nonfulfillment of this desire for presence by positing the actuality of being in an immobile container. So we find that another trace of the interval is legible in his work, the disavowed temporal thread entwining the present place of a body to the irrecuperable first dwelling. Irigaray describes this as an umbilical cord that man cannot sever (ESD, 49/E, 54).

She does not want to maintain this obscure figuration of the interval, because the interval is not thought in this scenario. She also wants to articulate ways in which woman functions as place in excess of maternity and to allow man to function as place too. Irigaray says she hopes that man and woman might sometimes occupy the same place (ESD, 35, 39–40, 54/E, 41–42, 45–46, 58). To achieve this, the specific status of the fetal–maternal relation must be addressed. Contra Aristotle, Irigaray suggests that place is so not much the mother's body but the membranes surrounding a fetus within the mother's body (ESD, 44/E, 49).

Even in his treatise on sexual generation, Aristotle does not discuss the membranes between mother and fetus. The womb is defined as the *topos* for the embryo (726a34–b1). If he did consider the placenta, it seems likely to me that he would maintain his definition of the womb as *topos*, because on his terms this fluid intermediary is not sufficiently immobile to circumscribe the fetus.[8]

Irigaray in "Place, Interval" does not directly describe the placenta as a modality of the interval. She develops this claim in a subsequent publication, an interview with the biologist Hélène Rouch called "On the Maternal Order" (JTN, 37–44/J, 45–54). Drawing on Rouch, Irigaray suggests that the placental relation between fetus and mother, far from a kind of fusion (the position she attributes to psychoanalysis), is "almost ethical" (*quasiment éthique*) (JTN, 38, 41/J, 46, 51). For her, the placental relation "represents one of these openings with regard to determinism, to vital or cultural closure, an opening which stems from female corporeal identity" (JTN, 38/J, 46).[9]

Rouch, like Irigaray, insists that the relationship between fetus and maternal body mediated by the placenta cannot be represented as a state of fusion nor as parasitic with the fetus figured as vampire devouring the mother's body from the inside (JTN, 39; 42–3/J, 48; 51). Rouch describes maternity as a "successful transplant." Unlike the transplanting of a limb, in which the recipient's body often rejects the transplant as a foreign organism, the placenta "negotiates" a relationship between the embryo, which is in part foreign (half of its genes are paternal), and the maternal body. The mother's body "recognizes" and accepts the placenta and the growing embryo *as other* within herself (JTN, 40–1/J, 48–50). As Rouch's research demonstrates, the placenta is fundamental to the success of a pregnancy.[10]

Is this another figuration of place as an interval? Where Aristotle's theory of *topos* collapses the placenta and the mucous membranes of the uterus, leaving mother and fetus in contiguity and woman fused to *topos*, Irigaray invokes the placenta as a threshold between the mother and the embryo. While this place is intimately related to the uterine mucosa of the mother's body, the placenta remains separate from it (JTN, 38/J, 46). Woman is no longer collapsible into place.

I have emphasized that the interval cannot be confined within the simplicity of the present. It is true that the placenta is a living tissue that operates for the term of pregnancy, and this can be presented as a (roughly) measureable period of time. Certainly, one of the goals of prenatal medicine is to calculate this time with precision. In Irigarayan terms, the placental relation gestures to the past experience of the mother, her relations with others and with her milieu, to her own prenatal life within her mother's body, and to her future, which is unknowable. The embryo is also virtually human—a boy or a girl—with an incalculable future. For Irigaray, the placental interval unfolds a living rhythm of times that cannot be mastered.

Irigaray does not spell out her reasons for using the qualifying word "almost" (*quasiment*) in her description of the complex interaction between embryo, placenta, and mother as "almost ethical" (JTN, 41/J, 51). I read "almost" in relation to her support for a woman's right to abortion (Whitford LI, 160). From this perspective, the interval between embryo and mother is not an intersubjective relation, because the fetus is not yet born and may never come to live as an other subject outside of her or his mother's body. Yet, in a virtual sense, the spatiotemporal relation enabled through the placenta is ethical, because the placental relation implies the possible futures of the mother and the fetus that may be born and come to live as a subject.[11]

It is not a symptom of nostalgia that leads Irigaray to privilege the fetal–maternal relation. On the contrary, she is engaged in a revaluation of motherhood beyond the construal of woman-place as the envelope for man-embryo. To think the placenta as an interval between woman and fetus is to articulate pregnancy as a function of her body rather than as woman's sole purpose. This prepares for the possibility of thinking woman as place in multiple senses; motherhood must be a component of female corporeal identity rather than a priority of it (JTN, 88/J, 110).

MUCUS

Perhaps the most important modality of interval for articulation of female subjectivity in Irigaray is the mucus. She suggests that the mucus is crucial to articulating woman as a multiple place and to thinking sexual difference nonhierarchically. The mucus has many senses in Irigaray's oeuvre, though strictly speaking the word "many" is inadequate here, for mucus is not quantifiable. Mucus is "in subtraction from the order of number" ESD, 110/E, 107).[12] (The incalculable status of the mucus has some affinity with Bergson's account of the qualitative multiplicities of duration, although we must not go too far here, as his qualitative multiplicities are posited as purely temporal, while the mucus is extensive and enduring. Irigaray's mucus is a threshold of sexual difference, while Bergson presents his qualitative multiplicities as sexually neutral.)

Mucus is known by both sexes in the "prenatal loving night" of the womb (ESD, 109/E, 107). In this context, mucus refers to the uterine mucosa and has an intimate relationship with the placental modality of the interval. Mucus thus serves as a fluid membrane between the placenta and the maternal body. Where the placenta is distinguished from the embryo's body and the mother's body, mucus is figured as an aspect of a pregnant woman's body. But woman's mucus is not restricted to a maternal function. Irigaray argues that mucus is particularly important in constituting woman's relationship to herself as place independent of pregnancy. Characteristically, Irigaray does not articulate precise thresholds of mucus in relation to woman. She seems to be describing the mucus that resides within and that sometimes flows from woman's vagina and from her mouth. She suggests provocatively that the mucus is the place of the soul of woman (ESD, 109/E, 107). It is difficult not to read this remark in relation to the Aristotle's description of the immaterial aspect of semen as divine. Where his semen transcends the sensible, Irigaray's mucus remains as a fluid related the corporeality of woman. And where Aristotle celebrates semen's divinity as the moving cause of a (male) child, Irigaray insists that mucus is not the cause of a product of *any* kind (737a7–10; Lloyd 1968, 59–60; Irigaray ESD, 111/E, 108).

Mucus has no *telos*. Irigaray writes:

> Never merely something available, never merely a material for some hand or some tool to use to construct a piece of work. And equally something that cannot possibly be denied. That always leaves a trace behind [*Il en reste toujours quelque chose*]: nostalgia for a return to the womb, a wound seeking a place deeper than the skin, a quest for a way into or out of the self and the other, for an encounter with the other which is always in excess of situation and expectation [*d'une recontre avec l'autre dont le terrain ou l'échéance font toujours défaut, etc*]. Impossible to suppress or forget entirely, without trace [*sans traces de lui*], it is only in an *act* that the mucous perceives and loves itself without thesis, without position outside itself. The potency achieves "its" act which is never set in a finished piece of work [*La puissance accomplit "son" acte, qui ne se pose jamais en oeuvre achevée*]. Always *partly open* [*entrouvert(e)*]. Never amounts simply to consumption [*la consummation*]. To producing some child. While serving love,

respiration, song, without ever taking hold of itself as such [*sans jamais se saisir comme tel*]. [Translation modified][13] (ESD, 111/E, 108)

In this extraordinary passage, Irigaray contends that the mucus has multiple thresholds—it serves love, respiration, song without ever taking hold of "itself." Mucus confounds immobility and the inside/outside opposition inscribed in the Aristotelian theory of place. It *is* in the very passage of becoming and is always partly open (*entrouvert[e]*). The mucus has no permanence and yet gestures toward temporal relations in radical excess of the present passage of its becoming. The mucus is sensible-transcendental. In stark contrast to Aristotle's presentation of *topos*, Irigaray's mucus cannot be contained within a definition.

I have emphasized that the mucus is particularly important to establishing woman as a place for herself. The material aspect of woman's mucus is not strictly reducible to her body—mucus is a bodily fluid—but the mucus allows woman to establish a relation with the placenta and the embryo growing inside her during pregnancy and to articulate intersubjective relationships with others through song, respiration, and love (ESD, 109, 111/E, 107, 108).

That the man's body might be conceived as a threshold of the mucus also deserves consideration. While Irigaray does not say so explicitly, man's respiration and song obviously require mucus as well. In this context, perhaps, man's saliva can be construed as a modality of mucus.[14] If man also has thresholds to the mucus, which I think he must, his relation to the mucus must be distinguished from woman's, for he does not have a vaginal threshold of mucus or the capacity to grow uterine mucosa. In other words, each sex has a different relation to the interval.

I have argued that the interval—mucus, placenta—"always remains in play as place, or the possibility of place" (ESD, 48/E, 53). This construal of place diverges starkly from Aristotle's concept of *topos*; Irigaray's interval is not circumscribed as a present limit; the interval is a sensible, porous, and mobile threshold to pasts and to futures that cannot be recuperated or anticipated or said to have being. The interval remains in radical excess of calculation and definition in the inflexible form of a traditional concept.

CARNAL INTERVAL(S)

By reconceiving *topos* as the interval, Irigaray articulates place so that it is no longer collapsible into woman's body. There are intervals that emerge from female corporeality, but these intervals are not reducible to her body. The interval is a multiple threshold that is by no means peculiar to the female sex; I have suggested that man's saliva might be conceived as mucus.

Irigaray is particularly concerned with thinking the interval as a generative relation between man and woman. In this context, some of her readers have charged her with prescribing a normative heterosexuality that excludes other kinds of sexual relationships (Butler in FSD, 28).[15] Most notoriously, perhaps, Judith Butler has suggested that Irigaray's work should be situated in "heterosexuality studies." This is a reductive assessment of Irigaray. While her focus on heterosexuality works at times to efface homosexual carnalities, Irigaray's revaluation of carnality offers important insights not only for heterosexuality but also for reconceiving lesbian and gay sex. These insights move beyond some violent dichotomies that too few queer theorists have questioned: activity and passivity, and outside and inside.[16] These dichotomies perpetuate sexual violence and must be overcome.

Irigaray's motivations are not straightforwardly heterosexist. She prioritizes the interval between woman and man because she is primarily concerned with elaborating a nonhierarchical relationship between the sexes. This nonhierarchical formulation is necessary because philosophy has been articulated as phallocentrism and predicated on the exclusion of the maternal-feminine, a violent figuration that renders impossible the conceptualization of woman as place for herself. The failure to think and live the interval of sexual difference has disastrous consequences in sexual life. "Its" obfuscation is intimately related to the widespread and continuing violence of rape and abuse carved into, and even formative of, the bodies and subjectivities of girls, women, men, boys, and the intersexed.

The interval between the sexes is not construed only in terms of carnality. Heterosocial relationships are elaborated in her work through a generative interval, and the interval is conceived also as a threshold in same-sex relations, sexual or otherwise.[17] This is explicit in a recent work, *Sharing the World* (2008), where Irigaray argues that her formulation of sexuate intersubjectivity should not be mistaken as a program for eroticism. She posits the sexuate relation in which each sex is able to respect the other as a different subject, with a different relationship to the world and a different relationship to herself or to himself. To privilege the erotic as the primary dimension of the relationship between woman and man runs the risk of eliding the irreducibility of the interval between sexes, the threshold that must be maintained in order to respect the difference between them.[18] This might seem to contradict the focus on sexuality in "Place, Interval." I prefer to read her warning against the privilege of eroticism in *Sharing the World* as a shift in emphasis. Sexual difference exceeds carnal relations. The task of articulating nonhierarchical ethics necessarily involves rethinking carnality, but this task is a dimension of engendering sexual difference rather than its exclusive impetus.

The placenta is a modality of the interval between the mother's uterine mucosa and the embryo; the embryo, of course, can be male or female. While Irigaray frequently discusses the mucus in the context of heterosexual coitus (more on this in a moment), mucus is especially significant in thinking through woman's relationship to herself as place. The mucus is also crucial for thinking lesbian sex.

Irigaray suggests that, if woman is thought as a multiple place through the interval, "the sexual *act*" (*l'*acte *sexuel*)—heterosexual coitus—would no longer be construed as a nostalgic and doomed act in which man strives to return to his first dwelling. She writes:

> The sexual *act* would turn into an act where the other restores [*me redone*] new form, birth, incarnation to the self. Instead [*Au lieu*] of bringing about the body's downfall, it participates in the body's renaissance. And there is no equivalent act in this sense. Most divine of acts. Whereby man makes woman feel her body as place. Not only her vagina and her womb but her body. He situates her within her body and within a macrocosm, releasing her potential [*éventuelle*] adherence to the cosmic through her participation in a microsociety. [Translation modified] (ESD, 51/E, 55)

Here, heterosexual coitus is presented as an "act" in which man and woman engender an intersubjective relationship with one another. Their bodies are not fused together; on the contrary, their lovemaking generates an interval between them that gives birth to both woman and man and establishes them as a couple or a "microsociety" that is an aspect of the macrocosm. Through the intimacy of coitus with her male lover, woman's multiple thresholds of place—her bodily identity, her vagina and her womb—are affirmed *and* generated by man. He releases woman from the potential confusion of her body with the universe. Man and woman's experiences of "the sexual act" are irreducible. For man, heterosexual coitus occurs outside of his body and within his lover's body, and he reconstructs his own body in the act of engendering the body of his female lover.[19] In contrast, woman experiences herself as an open container:

> Woman, insofar as she is a container, is never closed [*fermée*]. Place is never closed [*clos*]. The limits touch themselves while still remaining open [*Les limites se retouchent tout en restant ouvertes*]. . . There are two touches between the limits; and these are not the same; the touch of one's body at the threshold [*dedans-dehors*]; the touch of the contained other. [Translation modified] (ESD, 51/E, 55–56)

There are a number of problems with Irigaray's formulation. As Mary Beth Mader has asked, why should an act that is by definition heterosexual have "pride of place" as "*the* sexual act" (Mader 2003, 371)? Irigaray's description of "the sexual act" as the "most divine of acts" is also troubling. It relegates all forms of homosexual carnality to a subordinate position in relation to heterosexual coitus. And describing this act as "the most divine" also effaces the importance of other kinds of sexual acts between heterosexuals.

I have another objection to Irigaray's account of "the sexual act." Her description elides the activity of woman's sex(es) in heterosexual coitus. Irigaray focuses on man's active role in engendering woman's body and in re-creating his own body. Woman's activity is not directly considered, at least in these passages. This allows for the persistence of the traditional active–passive dichotomy that we have seen in Aristotle's designation of woman as passive in copulation (1149b32).

While these particular passages do not address the activity of woman in "the sexual act," there is a more interesting maneuver in "Place, Interval," the moment when Irigaray suggests that woman never was especially passive in heterosexual coitus (ESD, 44/E, 49). Dwelling inside a cunt is by no means a straightforwardly "active" experience. To be enveloped by the body of a lover is also an act in which the enveloped one feels vulnerable. In this context, Irigaray contends that, in nonhierarchical sexual difference, "the sexual act" would become an act in which woman gives form to man or, more precisely, to his penis. "She gives form to the male sex (organ) and sculpts it from within. She becomes the container and the active *place* of the sexual act" (emphasis in original; ESD, 43/E, 49). In light of this remark, it is possible to reread Irigaray's account of heterosexual coitus in the passages cited above as an act in which each sex incarnates the body of the other. The role of each lover remains irreducible, for woman engenders man from within herself, while man engenders woman from outside of himself.

Despite the overtly heterosexual orientation of Irigaray's description of "the sexual act" and her tendency to focus on coitus in particular, there are valuable lessons to draw from her account of carnality in "Place, Interval." The interval generated between woman and man in heterosexual lovemaking is not reducible to a product. Irigaray is not discussing sexual generation; she is describing the emergence of sexual difference through heterosexual coitus. Her description of this act as "the most divine of acts" should be read in relation to her thinking on the mucus, which is, among other things, a subversion of Aristotle's description of semen as divine (737a7–10). That is to say, when Irigaray describes heterosexual coitus as "the most divine of acts," she is praising the times when a passage to the mucus is engendered (ESD, 48/E, 53). This passage is an opening of nonhierarchical sexual difference. What is generated is not a product that can be presented and is not reducible to a particular bodily fluid. Sexual difference engenders a relationship between two irreducible beings—woman and man—and this relationship is not created once and for all; sexual difference must be ceaselessly rearticulated. Each articulation of this relationship (in this instance, the passage to the mucus) overflows presentation. In this sense, every attempt to define sexual difference fails, for sexual difference is discernible only in intervals—fluid traces that do not lend themselves to symbolization in the form of concepts.

Mader challenges the way in which Irigaray presents woman's experience of heterosexual lovemaking inside herself and man's experience of this act outside of himself. For Mader, "it is astonishing to have to point out that routinely men and women enter each other in making love; one would have to exclude from lovemaking the human kiss, among other human favourites" (2003, 371). As Mader realizes, Irigaray's position on this distinction is also undermined by other aspects of her thinking, "given that she frequently articulates much more nuanced, complex and illuminating thought on the topic of sexuality" (2003, 371). Irigaray's writing on the mucus is relevant here, for the figuration of the mucus works to undo any straightforward distinction between "inside" and "outside." Mucus is uncontainable; mucus has no permanence and respects no borders; mucus *is* only in an act that never accomplishes "itself." The passage to the mucus is not restricted to flows from woman's vagina. The mucus serves love, respiration, and song (ESD, 111/E, 108).

Although Irigaray does not say so, I think lesbian carnalities also function as thresholds to the mucus and the possibility of a non-hierarchical relation of difference between women. For Irigaray, these relations are not ontological (2000d, 159–60). While I agree that sexual difference renders the other of the other sex stranger to me in sexuate terms than the other of my own sex, I do not think that the interval between women (or the interval between men) is secondary to the interval between woman and man. They are qualitatively different articulations of the rhythm of interval. In Irigarayan terms, homosexuality is coherent as homosexuality only if we acknowledge at least two sexes instead of one.

The penultimate page of "Place, Interval" provides what I regard as a compelling description of the interval(s) in carnality. In this passage, heterosexual erotics are no longer confined to traditional coitus or to distinctions between the inside and the outside, and the enduring dichotomy between activity and passivity is put out of play:

> In love, it would be fitting [*il coviendrait*] if the parts of the whole—the union of man and woman—enveloped one another *mutually* and

> did not destroy one another's envelopes. How fitting if the journeys of going-returning [*les trajets aller-retour*] from one to the other became places for enveloping. If the portions of place traversed in order to distance and to return [*s'éloigner et revenir*] were to become spaces-times [*espaces-temps*] that mutually recovered and were not eliminated, annihilated, used up to provide fuel for other kinds of locomotion, or transformed into voids, separations, rather than bridges [*passerelles*]. Between the one and the other, there should be mutual enveloping in movement. [Translation modified] (ESD, 54/E, 58)

The whole engendered in this heterosexual erotics is not a closed whole. The body of each lover is irreducible to the other and remains open to the reserves of the lovers' past experiences and to the emergence of space-times that cannot be anticipated. Woman is no longer the sole container in coitus. Man also serves as an envelope for his lover. Each body is mobile, and the passage of each body articulates an interval that entwines with the interval engendered by the body of the other. Through this relation, the lovers generate an interval between them, which is their place, a mobile, porous place that cannot be closed.[20]

Strictly speaking, the temporality of the interval between the lovers is not an effect of the intervals that each lover engenders in the passage toward and movements away from the other. The interval is the very stake (*enjeu*) of desire impelling woman to generate a threshold for man and impelling man to engender a threshold for woman. In this sense, the interval between woman and man is constitutive of the emergence of different thresholds to the interval specific to each sex.

Irigaray does not develop an account of how man's morphology might be reconceived as an envelope that receives woman or another man in carnal relations.[21] She does point out that traditional figurations of masculine morphology are not readily amenable to serving as receptive places for the body of a lover (ESD, 39/E, 45). Drawing on Mader, we can argue that man's mouth is a vessel for woman or another man and that man's saliva can be construed as a modality of the mucus. There is another receptive vessel within man's body that

Irigaray does not discuss and of which heterosexual men are infamously fearful—the rectum. In this context, we might object to Irigaray's claim that male morphology is not constituted as receptive in Western phallocentric cultures. But I think that Irigaray is describing the traditional figuration of masculine morphology, which disavows the rectum and the mouth as receptive openings. To the extent that man's rectum figures in discourse, it is figured as a reviled and dreaded place, while man's mouth is rarely symbolized as a receptive place.[22]

Mortensen addresses the morphological status of man's rectum in an impressive essay that calls for a radical reappraisal of passivity (2002, 7–19). Drawing on Leo Bersani's famous article "Is the Rectum a Grave?" (1989), she argues that the "passive, inactive and penetrated position" is the most denigrated and feared position in the West, whether you are a man or a woman.[23] Bersani suggests that the AIDS-afflicted dying gay man is emblematic in this context, for his rectum signifies the human dread of mortality: "By means of a metonymical displacement, the rectum becomes a grave and the dying male homosexual comes to signify death, a space and a figure that must be ostracized from the narcissistic image of the active, potent and dynamic Western subject" (Mortensen 2002, 17).

I agree with Bersani and Mortensen's claim that the rectum of the gay man dying of AIDS is the most dreaded position in contemporary Western culture. However, I do not think that the "passive, inactive and penetrated position" of a man is symmetrical with woman's position as "penetrated" in coitus. The revulsion toward the infected and sick gay man does not derive only from a fear of AIDS.[24] Rather, dread is exhibited toward any "passive" gay man precisely because he has constituted his body as a vessel for his lover and renounced the privileged phallic activity supposedly proper to his sex. Woman's (alleged) passivity is perhaps less denigrated because her passivity is at least in keeping with the traditional figuration of her morphology.[25]

Mortensen's demand to rethink passivity is important, and Irigaray's "Place, Interval" must be a central text in the elaboration of this difficult task (Mortensen 2002, 17). Irigaray's essay is a sustained engagement with passivity and with the transvaluation of passivity's denigration in the Western tradition. Let me recall Irigaray's critical description of passivity in Aristotle discussed earlier in this chapter. Irigaray suggests that woman never was especially passive in heterosexual coitus (ESD, 44/E, 49). Woman's alleged passivity is a phallocentric sham effacing the activity of maternity. I argued that the most passive positions are the place of the embryo inside the mother's body and the place of an infant suckling on the maternal breast. These relationships have not been thought through. Woman-place collapses into the womb-vagina, which is *presented* as passive in phallocentric figurations of heterosexual coitus. Irigaray argues that woman-place is obliquely in a position of active envelopment, and hence the ambivalent status of castration and of the English "obscenities" "cunt" and "suck." The passivity attributed to the gay man's rectum recalls the womb-vagina, but, because his body is not "supposed" to be a vessel, his "passivity" is even more reviled than woman's.

To my knowledge, Irigaray is the only thinker to suggest that a vessel is an "active place" for the generation of intimacy (ESD, 43/E, 49). While she devotes her attention primarily to heterosexual coitus, her engagement with this problematic has fascinating implications for lesbian sex and other kinds of envelopments. In the wake of her argument, the body of a woman who is entered by her lover is not passive. The one who constitutes her body as an envelope does not become a mere hole to be thrust into by a tongue, fingers, or some other kind of body. For a place of receptivity to be generated, the one who offers her body gives place to the body of the other. These places are mobile and act on the bodies they envelop. In this sense, any straightforward opposition between activity and passivity unravels.

What else does Irigaray's thinking on carnality have to offer theorists concerned with articulating lesbianism? It suggests that we should not privilege a woman as phallic or "active" in opposition to the "passivity" of her lover. I am not sure the categories of activity and passivity have ever been particularly salient given that lesbian sex routinely involves both lovers entering and exiting multiple thresholds of place. Each lover is capable of engendering mucus from her mouth, the pores of her skin, and her vagina. When a woman enters an envelope offered to her by her lover, the woman who enters this place of intimacy is bound to this place in a particular way. Her relation to the envelope her lover gives her is entwined with the sexed morphology of her own body and is morphologically substitutable with the body of her lover.

The inside–outside distinction is important to many sexual acts and must not be construed dichotomously. At the very least, the "interior" position that phallocentrism derides as "penetrated" must be revalued. Irigaray's inscriptions of the inside-outside distinction move away from dichotomy toward an interlacing of each term through the generation of an interval. This is evident in her predilection for the expression "inside–outside" (*dedans-dehors*), or "threshold" as it is usually translated in English, another inscription of interval (ESD, 51/E, 56).

Irigaray also seeks to articulate carnality in excessive terms that cannot be resolved to the conventional fixation on the genitalia of women and men. She has famously suggested that "woman has sex organs more or less everywhere" (*la femme a des sexes un peu partout*) (TS, 25/CS, 28). Male morphology requires rethinking beyond the anxious attention devoted to the erect penis pervasive in mainstream Western culture. Drawing on Irigaray, the male sex might be reconceived as an open envelope with multiple thresholds to welcome the other.

For Irigaray the difference between the sexes is irreducible. This means that the multiple thresholds of place in man and the multiple thresholds of place in woman are not interchangeable. These differences between the sexes should not be conceived in terms of lack. In an ethic of nonhierarchical sexual difference, the differences between woman and man's morphologies should be affirmed and valued as specific to each sex.[26]

YES, YES

"Place, Interval" addresses the articulation of two sexes—woman and man. This is unsurprising—*An Ethics of Sexual Difference* was published in French in 1983, several years before the emergence of queer theory and two decades before the arrival of transgender theory. To my knowledge, Irigaray continues to marginalize the possibility of more than two sexes among human beings and the fact that sexuation combines the genetic material of male and female. For instance, in a particularly careless remark, she declares inaccurately that "the whole of humankind is composed of only men and women and of nothing else" (1996, 47). In the face of the ongoing persecution of intersexed people in the West (such as sex-reassignment surgery performed on infants), the affirmation of intersexed bodies is urgent. The carnal, philosophical, legal, political, and ethical struggles faced by transgender women and men must also be supported in thinking and living an ethics of sexual difference.

ENGENDERING SEXUATE NATURE: BETWEEN MATTER AND FORM

Irigaray's dialogue with Aristotle in *An Ethics of Sexual Difference* should be read in relation to her first engagement with his corpus in "How to Conceive of (a) Girl?" In *An Ethics of Sexual Difference* she finds a way to rearticulate the matter-and-form relation beyond the extreme violence of the hylomorphism described with such force in "How to Conceive (of) a Girl?"

In the mid-eighties text, Irigaray foregrounds the interval as the generative threshold from which each sex is articulated in relation to the other. This maneuver effects a transvaluation of the matter-and-form relationship (IR, 167–68, 170/ESD, 7–8, 12/E, 15–16, 19). Matter and form are not conceived exclusively as the components that make up sexed subjects, they are constitutive of all perceptible bodies. Yet the tradition has persistently posited these concepts in a sexed hierarchy: matter is feminine and form is masculine. In this sense, rethinking sexual difference beyond hierarchy is already implicated in rethinking the matter–form relation.

Let me return to the conception of *physis*. For Aristotle, *physis* is made up of both *hylē* and *morphē*. These two concepts do not have an equal share in defining the being (*ousia*) of *physis*. Form (*morphē, eidos*) is more properly said to be *physis* than matter, for it is the very source (*archē*) of movement (*kinēseōs*) in things, which defines *physis* as what it is (*ti esti*) (193a35–b4).[27] Matter, by contrast, has no specificity. It is the underlying substrate (*hypokeimon*) of a thing that can be said to have being only when it abides with form. In the absence of form, matter is characterized by privation (*sterēsis*) or not-being (192a4–5; 192a31).

Aristotle conceptualizes the emergence of *physis* in sexualized terms. Matter desires (*orexis*) the active principle of form, and this yearning impels form to destroy (*pthora*) the privation in matter and to create *physis*. Form is masculine and what it destroys—privation—is female (192a16–23). In Irigaray's argument in *An Ethics of Sexual Difference*, Aristotle's concept of privation is a trace of the interval, the very stake (*enjeu*) of desire (IR, 167; ESD, 7–8, 48/E, 15, 53). Here, the interval is conceived as a lack in matter that masculine form annihilates in order to create a being that has its source in *physis*.

Yet the murderous scenario structuring Aristotle's *hylomorphism* is much more complicated than this. As I argued in Chapter One, Irigaray's "How to Conceive of (a) Girl?" demonstrates that the female sex is not only privation, she is also matter (S, 165/SA, 206). This is pronounced in his treatise on sexual reproduction, where woman's menstrual fluid (*katamenia*) is classed as *prōte hylē* and grudgingly acknowledged as one the four causes in the creation of a human being. The other three causes—the moving cause (form), the efficient cause, and the final cause—are all masculine (Lloyd AGS, 59–60). Aristotle downplays the contribution of *hypokeimenon*. For instance, he names the father as the moving cause of his child in *Metaphysics* 5 but neglects to mention the mother when he describes the primary substratum (1013a24–33). In *Physics* 2, woman's contribution to reproduction is erased, "the form [*morphē*] of the human [*anthrōpou*] is his nature [*physis*]. For human is born from human [*gignetai gar ex anthrōpōi anthrōpōs*]" (translation modified, 193b12).

If woman is matter to man's form, then the moment when form acts on matter to create a being in actuality (*entelechia*) would seem to domesticate the female sex as a subordinate partner in the matter–form hierarchy. This is arguably an improvement on woman's status as privation, where she is killed off completely by form, at least in Aristotle's argument. But what is more significant for Irigaray is that the female sex is both matter *and* privation. Woman is denigrated in both instances. Yet, by functioning as potential being in one case and as a lack in being in the other, woman violates Aristotle's most privileged principle, the law of noncontradiction. Woman is both privation and potentiality. By virtue of occupying this no-man's-land, she is *neither one nor the other* (S, 165/SA, 206).

This paradoxical entanglement is extraordinarily troubling for the hierarchical figuration of matter and form in Aristotle. It betrays the inextricability of privation and matter, and this means form's proclaimed annihilation of the lack in being is by no means secure. The not-being of woman-*sterēsis* threatens to engulf the actuality (*entelechia*) of form precisely at the moment when form is supposed to act on woman-*hylē* and create *physis*. By virtue of woman's uncontainability, she is a threat.

In the wake of this contradiction, Irigaray posits the maternal-feminine as the secret source of *physis* (S, 161/SA, 201). It is true that the maternal-feminine and the interval are not present in Aristotle, but the fact that woman is both matter and privation gives away the grounding status of the maternal-feminine and the interval as the opening from which *physis* is born (*physein*). Because the maternal-feminine and the interval cannot be resolved *by* or *in* being, they do not function as the stable ground for his system. On the contrary, the maternal-feminine and the interval are the abyss into which his concept of *physis* plunges.

In "How to Conceive (of) a Girl?" Irigaray demonstrates that the maternal-feminine is the omnipotent source of *physis*. This amounts to identifying a collapse of the A/Not-A dichotomy in the Aristotelian account of *physis*. The law of excluded middle between form and privation is unraveled by woman's excessive status as both privation and matter. Privileging the maternal-feminine is not Irigaray's overall aspiration, for the maternal-feminine is confused with the interval, and these formless figures have no specificity. In this sense, "How to Conceive (of) a Girl?" closes at an impasse. Irigaray puts Aristotle's *hylomorphism* out of play but does not offer a transvaluation of matter and form. "Place, Interval" and the introduction to *An Ethics of Sexual Difference* return to this problematic and find a way to rearticulate matter and form nonhierarchically. Irigaray posits a generative interval between them, which is figured as the very condition of their emergence (IR, 167–68; ESD, 7–8, 37/E, 15–6, 43).

Chapter Two argued that Aristotle's thinking on the relationship between *topos* and substance (*ousia*) is beset by an aporia, which betrays difference at the heart of the identity of his highest category. Substance is the species-form (*eidos*) and is defined in *Metaphysics* 7 as one (*en to*) (1037b25–28; Lear 1988, 286–87). Of all of the categories, substance is the only order of being that is said to be independent of everything else (1028a35). Yet in *Physics* 4, Aristotle affirms that the being of form in the definition (*eidos en tos logos*) is a modality of being in something else (*allo en allōi*). The most basic (*kuriōtaton*) way in which one thing is said to be in another (*allo en allōi*) is to be *en topōi* (210a15–210a25). Place in Aristotle designates a contiguous situation between two sensible bodies that are different in being (*heteron to einai*), a contained body and the first unchangeable limit that it surrounds (*periechonotos peras akinēton prōtōn*) (210b16; 212a20–21). If this relation precedes the being of form in the definition (*eidos en tos logos*), then substance cannot be one (*en ti*). The ideality of substance is brought into question here also if it is subordinate to a sensible relation.

We are finally in a position to understand how the aporetic relationship between envelope and things is one of or, rather, *the* aporia of Aristotelianism and of the philosophical systems that have evolved from it (IR, 169/ESD, 10/E, 17). *Topos* designates a relation between two sensible bodies that have their source in *eidos*, the *ousia* of things. Yet the unity (*en ti*) of *ousia* is predicated on the difference between these two bodies, so how can the matter–form relationship of either the envelope or the thing in place be conceptualized?

In Aristotle's metaphysics, this aporia is insurmountable; it betrays irreducible difference at the heart of his ontology. Difference in his theory of *topos* can be thought as a *present* difference only between two bodies that stand in a contiguous relationship to one another. Irigaray does not seek to surmount the aporetic relationship between envelope and things, for an aporia is an opening to thinking the interval of sexual difference, and the interval cannot be mastered or presented to thought as such.

This chapter has addressed the aporia between envelope and things in relation to the analogy, between place and sexual difference, that Irigaray identifies in Aristotle's theory of *topos*. According to her critical description, man or, more precisely, man-embryo is the thing circumscribed by place. Woman is both place and the very collapse of place, because she is entangled with the disavowed interval (*diastēma*). In this sense, while Aristotle's account of *topos* is supposed to apply to all perceptible bodies, the terms in which it is articulated are anthropomorphic. More precisely, this anthropomorphism is a phallomorphism.

Aristotle's *hylomorphism* is obliquely dependent on the aporia between envelope and things as well. At first glance, the sexed hierarchy underwriting the figuration of a body *en topōi* does not mesh readily with the phallocentrism Irigaray discerns in his *hylomorphism*. In "How to Conceive (of) a Girl?" man is form and woman is both matter and privation, and in the *Physics* Aristotle takes pains to distinguish both form and matter from his concept of *topos*. In Irigaray's transvaluation, place becomes the interval and the interval is no longer an independent gap between corporeal bodies (*diastēma*) that has no existence. Nor is the interval the privation (*sterēsis*) of form. The interval is a corporeal and transcendental threshold (*dedans-dehors*) that entwines the body of woman in relation to the body of man. What does this have to do with matter and form?

Hylomorphism is phallomorphism—woman is matter and privation, and man is form. Together, these concepts make up Aristotle's *physis*. Irigaray does not maintain the hierarchical sexuation of this scenario, but, because these concepts have been articulated in terms of a sexed hierarchy, she is obliged to rethink their sexuation. Form is no longer male, and matter is not exclusively female. Privation is radically transvalued; this lack in being is celebrated as a generative interval (IR, 167–68/ESD, 7–8/E, 15–16). I think her argument suggests that each sex is made up of matter, form, and an interval between the matter and form specific to each sex. These components constitute two irreducible natures: woman and man.[28]

The description I have just provided is misleading if it is read to suggest that woman and man are conceived as sexually marked individuals that have being prior to their coming together and moving away through the interval between them. For Irigaray, man and woman are not cognizable prior to the articulation of the interval. The emergence of the interval is the very condition on which woman and man emerge as sexed beings. Each subject is engendered in the relation to the other through the interval.

This argument can be read as a response to the aporia, the aporia between envelope and things, that Aristotelianism cannot acknowledge. A man, for instance (what Aristotle calls *physis*), is cognizable as a man only through his relationship to another envelope that remains irreducible, woman. Irigaray rewrites the terms of this aporia so that the relationship is between two envelopes—man and woman. Each sex has the potential to function as a receptive place to receive and welcome the other. The two envelopes do not fit together; each sex has an irreducible relation to the interval, an excess that maintains double dissymmetry between them. In Irigaray's thinking, the difference between woman and man is not given once and for all. *The interval always remains in play.* In other words, the aporia between the envelopes remains open to reconfigurations that cannot be calculated. If the interval is essentially open to the articulation of relations that do not have being, then the interval cannot be consumed in the function of generating nonhierarchical relations between woman and man. The interval is the threshold of the possibility of relations beyond sexual difference.

I think this is why the rewriting of matter and form is so abstract in *An Ethics of Sexual Difference*. For Irigaray, matter and form are brought together by the interval, the place of desire. Matter is shaped by form, but matter is by no means subordinate in this formation. What impels the form is not a lack in matter but the generative interval *between* form and matter. And the interval always remains in play, ceaselessly inducing new formations and reformations. Matter and form entwine with each other in attractions, tensions, and acts that are never accomplished (IR, 167–68; ESD, 8, 48, 49/E, 15–16, 53, 54). This means that the matter-interval-forms engendered through the interval are not static. The interval is the place of the past, of a body's (conscious or unconscious) memory of previous incarnations; the interval also impels material transformations that cannot be anticipated (IR, 167–68/ESD, 8/E, 16). In this sense, the interval—place—"would in some way be the 'nature' of matter and form, the habitat in which both wed without ceasing, and in their extension. To infinity" (ESD, 37/E, 43).[29] The implications of her argument are not restricted to human beings or to sexual difference beyond the human. Irigaray's thinking of the interval is a thinking of difference as the motor of becoming-and-being.

To argue that the interval gives place to relations of alterity that cannot be anticipated is to suggest that the interval is multiple. Yet, on the other hand, Irigaray emphasizes that the interval is "in subtraction from the order of number" (ESD, 110/E, 107). This is an aphoristic claim that demands more attention than I have been able to give it in this chapter. Irigaray's thinking on the nature of this multiple threshold is oblique. I believe her articulation of this nonnumerical formulation is, in some ways, closely resonant with Bergson's thinking on duration as a qualitative multiplicity. It is to his sustained engagement with the specific dynamics of duration that I turn in the second part of this book.

PART II

Becoming

4. Dualism in Bergson

I had been aware that duration is measured by the trajectory of a body in motion and that mathematical time is a line; but I had not yet observed that this operation contrasts radically with all other processes of measurement, for it is not carried out on an aspect of or an effect representative of what one wishes to measure, but on something which excludes it. The line one measures is immobile, time is mobility. The line is made, it is complete; time is what is happening, and more than that, it is what causes everything to happen [*La ligne est du tout fait, le temps est ce qui se fait, et même ce qui fait que tout se fait*]. The measuring of time never deals with duration as duration; what is counted is only a certain number of extremities of intervals [*intervalles*], or moments, in short, virtual halts in time.

BERGSON CM, 12/O, 1254–55

BERGSON'S PHILOSOPHY OF DURATION is important for elaborating the temporality of the interval. In stark contrast to Aristotle's inability to affirm the interval openly, Bergson privileges a concept of the interval. For Bergson, this concept is the threshold of duration and intuition, the method he believes philosophy must pursue in order to become a rigorous discipline capable of knowing life. Yet this divergence between Aristotle and Bergson is not as stark as it might at first appear. Bergson's intuitive approach to the interval of duration, like Aristotle's metaphysics, depends on a disavowed sexed hierarchy, which effaces the possibility of thinking the interval as the opening of sexual difference.

We have seen how Aristotle's philosophy figures sexual difference hierarchically; for example, in his misogynist figuration of the dualism between matter and form. But his debasement of the female sex is exceeded by traces of the maternal-feminine. These traces function not so much as a lack in opposition to a virile masculinity but as a nourishing resource on which Aristotle's thought depends unconsciously to articulate metaphysics. Specifically, the maternal-feminine ensures the relation or interval (*diastēma*) between terms in the theorization of *topos* and in the deduction of the identity of substance (*ousia*).

The recurrence of dualism in Bergson's method must be distinguished from the binary logic formalized by Aristotle. He conceives of dualism hierarchically. For Irigaray and Derrida, Aristotle's thinking instantiates violent hierarchies between a privileged concept (A) and its devalued opposite (Not-A). He affords no positive identity to what falls outside the proper borders of a concept (Irigaray S, 160–67/SA, 200–9; Derrida 1981, 41). Two pronounced examples of this in Aristotle are "man" and "white." Everything that does not belong to these concepts is rendered amorphous. For instance, man is opposed to woman or animal or the Deity, and white is opposed to black or to the privation of color. Drawing on Irigaray, I suggested that the opposition between the being of man and the not-being of woman is far less secure than Aristotle admits, for woman is also associated with the potentiality of matter, which means that she violates the law of noncontradiction. As Irigaray argues, woman is both being and not-being and equally neither one nor the other (S, 165/SA, 206).

In contrast to Aristotle's abandonment of the devalued side of a dichotomy to conceptual confusion, Bergson is rigorous in the articulation of both sides of a dualism. Deleuze suggests that Bergsonism is ultimately a monistic philosophy (Deleuze B, 29/BE, 20). Dualisms are deployed provisionally to establish distinctions between tendencies that are mixed up in the philosophical tradition; Bergson disentangles durational phenomena from homogeneous space in order to emphasize what is specific to time and what is specific to space. Once these two orders are defined rigorously, Bergson is able to reintegrate them into a monism in which the difference between pure extension and pure duration is conceived as a difference in temporal tension. While I am in partial agreement with Deleuze's reading, I contend that Bergson's tendency to dichotomize is more than a methodological step. His predilection for dualism can be read as symptomatic of a sexed hierarchy at the very heart of his open system.

The sexuation of Bergson's thought is betrayed in his use of metaphor and image. Life, duration, and consciousness are valorized with metaphors of paternity and images of erection and height, while the tendencies of space and matter are enmeshed with derogated images of the feminine. This is important in Bergson because images and metaphors are privileged in his method. He believes that language is spatial in essence, which means that he cannot present the intuition of duration as such. Therefore precise use of image and metaphor is often a better way to convey the mobility of real time, because images and metaphors can "suggest" the intuition of duration in a "direct vision" (Bergson CM, 43/O, 1285).

Despite the hierarchical sexuation at work in his project, Bergson's metaphysics is a significant resource for a feminist philosophy of the interval. He construes the interval as the opening from which time and space and the life–matter relation emerge. If I am right about the way in which a sexed hierarchy implicitly structures his thinking, feminist work on Bergson's interval is a fraught undertaking. It requires more than the odd footnote acknowledging his sexism.[1] We must evaluate the implications of the hierarchical sexuation at play in his philosophy and we must transvalue the sexed hierarchy in his work to generate a way to rethink Bergson's interval as the interval of sexual difference. That is the central task of Chapter Five. Drawing on Irigaray's critical description of metaphysics as phallocentrism, I argue that Bergson's deduction of consciousness as duration is predicated on the disavowal of a sexed hierarchy. To diagnose this hierarchy is the first step toward dismantling it. I suggest a way of rethinking his phallocentrism to articulate Bergson's interval as a sensible and transcendental difference that articulates a nonhierarchical relation between the sexes.

Bergsonism is by no means reducible to a philosophy of human consciousness. From this perspective, rewriting his interval of duration as the threshold of sexed intersubjectivity is reductionist. I take up the transhuman aspects of his project in Chapter Six, through a reading of his figuration of the life–matter relation. This is where his philosophy takes on a monistic orientation. I suggest that, despite the affirmation of monism, Bergson's life–matter relation remains entangled in a humanist sexed hierarchy. And yet in his work there are also tendencies that exceed this sexually violent scenario and that might enable a thinking of life and matter beyond the constraints of human being.

This chapter presents Bergson's dualism between space and duration under several aspects. I look at his critical description of how intellectual knowledge obscures the possibility of an intuitive philosophy of real time. Then I turn to his deduction of duration as the threshold of difference in *Time and Free Will*. I also analyze his account of the relationship between language and thought; this relationship is important to my reading of the sexuate stakes of Bergsonism. The difficult questions that arise from my claim that his thinking is entwined with a sexed hierarchy are largely deferred to the following chapters.

ATTENTION TO LIFE

According to Bergson, philosophy has repressed its humble beginnings by neglecting to consider the *relation* between metaphysics and the demands of human practical life. He argues that the dominant model of philosophical knowledge has been conceived as an apparatus of pure speculation, unencumbered by the ordinary requirements that confront humans in the sphere of action. What must be done to establish metaphysics as a truly precise discipline is to trace the genesis of thought as an instrument of action. Only then can philosophy begin to articulate what Bergson calls "pure" knowledge, or intuition.

For instance, in the opening pages of the *Metaphysics*, Aristotle specifies that philosophy is the most authoritative form of knowledge because it is not a science of production (982b12). It has no practical end or purpose other than the pursuit of wisdom; metaphysics is pursued purely for the sake of knowing.[2] Aristotle acknowledges that practical forms of knowledge precede the emergence of philosophy. He says it is only when almost all of the necessities of life are fulfilled that "men" (*anthrōpoi*) are free to think for pleasure's sake; that is, to engage in speculative thought (982b23–38). In Bergson's terms, the problem with Aristotle's formulation is that productive knowledge already determines speculation. Aristotle's neglect of the impact that the demands of practice have on the development of the intellect obscures the relation between metaphysics and practical thought. In Bergson's view, philosophy must clarify this relation; otherwise, metaphysics tends to engender knowledge that is relative to the requirements of action.

For Bergson, this is because the evolution of intellect is a particular response to imperatives that go beyond the human condition, although metaphysics has remained unaware of their importance. Animals and plants, from the most rudimentary to the most complex, are bound by the same demand: to fulfill their bodily needs. Before anything else, *all* forms of life are obliged to obtain food and shelter and seek protection from threats of injury and death. Bergson calls this the law of "attention to life" (*l'attention à la vie*) (MM, 173/O, 312).

By attributing primacy to the demands of life, Bergson hopes to give philosophy a foundation that precedes and exceeds the kinds of knowledge specific to humans. This principle, which is of fundamental importance to his thought as a whole, is perhaps the most pronounced gesture toward antihumanism in his oeuvre. Yet this gesture is also implicated in an anthropomorphic sexed hierarchy; the law of attention to life obliquely announces the primary dichotomy that pervades Bergson's oeuvre: the difference between life and nonlife. Chapter Five argues that traces of a hierarchical conception of sexual difference are the unavowed condition of this dichotomy. Life is inscribed with the privileges of seminal creativity and virility, while nonlife is characterized with metaphors of debased femininity.

Intellection, the dominant form of thought in common sense and philosophy, emerged in humans as the preeminent faculty for responding to life's demands.[3] The intellect does not engage with the environment to obtain pure knowledge but to select what is of interest in present perception. It is a highly motivated form of thought that, in radical contrast to Aristotle's belief, is precisely knowledge of production. For Bergson, intellection is not the only form of thought attainable in metaphysics. He believes there is another method of thinking that has a much broader orientation, intuition. Where intellect limits its scope to the preparation of action, intuition extends to the whole of living reality.

Given the extraordinary complexity of life, there are a myriad of problems confronting intuitive philosophy, which means that it cannot be pursued by a single method. For Bergson, then, intuition does not consist of a single act but an indefinite series of acts (CM, 184/O, 1416). These acts will vary depending on the problem under consideration. Intuition, like intellection, is a kind of action. It is radically different to the intellect, however, because it is an order of action that aims at no result other than the comprehension of life. Moreover, the data that intuition obtains cannot be enclosed in the static terms of results, because life is evolving. Intuition must remain open to the unforeseeable manifestations that life will take.

The primary objects of intuition are the recovery of real time and mobility, which have been obscured in our intellectual heritage. The word "object" is misleading here if an overly intellectual sense is attached to it. One meaning that Bergson ascribes to intuition is as an immediate awareness of duration, a kind of comprehension of change from within rather than from a perspective, which implies a separation between the mind and the object it conceptualizes.

Think of an object moving through space. For the intellect, the object exists outside of the mind. It can be viewed from different perspectives, and with each new perspective the movement will appear to the mind under a new aspect. The traversal of space by the object can be plotted with reference points, which change when the observing position is altered. The intellectual knowledge of this movement is thus relative to the perspective that the mind adopts toward the object. Bergson contends that there is another way to comprehend the moving object. Through an effort of intuition he can attribute to the mobile "an inner being" and imagine he is "inside the object itself" (*dans l'objet lui-même*). There is no need to construct axes in space to trace out lines symbolizing its mobility, since he is, in a certain sense, within the object. Bergson declares that his intuitive sympathy with the mobile gives him absolute knowledge. He says, "I have hold of an absolute" (*je tiendrai un absolu*) (CM, 159–60/O, 1394).

Bergson's comparison of the two different ways of conceiving of a moving object goes to the heart of his polemic against metaphysics. As we can see from his example, intellectual representation translates time and mobility into symbols: points, axes, and lines sketched onto a grid of space. These are the concepts of homogeneous space formalized in Euclidean geometry and still taught to schoolchildren. This order of space functions as a mental diagram for intellection. It gives humans a practical way of understanding the trajectory of an object but cannot reveal mobility itself. For Bergson, mobility and duration are radically different from the spatial phenomena represented in a diagram. What is needed is a sustained effort to think time without recourse to geometrical translation. Time must be thought in its specificity. This does not mean intuition must transcend space; what must be exceeded is the intellectual conception of space, a homogeneous medium in which humans plan their actions on things.

For Bergson, the spatialization of mobility effected by the intellect is indicative of much more than a decisive accident in the history of thought. Spatialization stems from the vital tendency to action that precedes the systematic formulations of the Greeks. He calls it "a latent geometry, immanent to our idea of space, which is the mainspring of our intellect and that which makes it work" (translation modified; CE, 211/O, 674). In other words, the projection of homogeneous calculable space, masquerading as an adequate measurement of time, is both the cause and the primary function of the intellect. For Bergson, the *structure* of human understanding demands the masking of duration. It enables us to delimit objects with clear and distinct outlines that are perfectly suited to facilitate our actions on them (CE, 211/O, 674).

Bergson's claim that spatialization derives from a vital human tendency is Eurocentric. The intellectual procedure in which a subject isolates objects as immobile and delineates them with clear outlines in homogeneous space is alien to many Aboriginal philosophies. For example, Irene Watson, a Nunga feminist legal scholar, describes Nunga ontology in these terms: "We are not merely on and in the land, we are of it, we speak as one voice of the Creation, the voice or song law. Land and people are one voice, one song" (Watson 2002, 7).

While Bergson's account of the obfuscation of duration by homogeneous space does not hold as a universal description of human knowledge, I think it is a salient description of the cover-up of mobility and time in Western thought. His critique demonstrates the need in Western philosophy for a method of thinking capable of grasping time.

THE OBLIVION OF DURATION

The surviving paradoxes of motion attributed to Zeno of Elea occupy an important place in Bergson's project of recovering real movement and duration. Zeno of Elea is afforded the dubious honor of inaugurating metaphysics with the elaboration of his famous paradoxes of motion and change (CM, 17/O, 1259). Zeno's postulates demonstrate the impossibility of understanding movement with the concepts of intellection. What Zeno does not say (and this is the point of Bergson's critique) is that movement might be thought without recourse to homogeneous space.

For instance, Zeno argues that an arrow will never reach its goal because it must first reach the halfway point in its journey. To make that part of the journey, the arrow would need to traverse an infinite number of points. If the arrow did somehow reach the midpoint of its destination, it would still have to pass through an indefinite series of positions to reach the halfway point between the middle of the passage and the final destination. Bergson argues that this logic confuses the movement of the arrow with the path it takes (MM, 192/O, 328). Our intellect imagines that, if we could arrest an instant in the journey of the arrow, it would have to be *in* a point of its path. But the path the arrow takes is no more than a retrospective projection by our intellect of a line drawn beneath the completed movement. The line drawn is immobile, whereas the arrow's movement is in duration. The instants we distinguish on the line are an illusion generated by our intellect, which is to say that duration cannot be conceived with instants; this would amount to constituting mobility with abstract "immobilities" juxtaposed in space (MM, 190/O. 326). That we can imagine the arrow in one of the earlier points reveals that it might stop at an earlier place, not that it has to.

For Bergson, the intellect and common sense are justified in constructing movement with these motionless concepts because they function as practical guides to our conduct. "The duration wherein we see ourselves acting, and which it is useful that we should see ourselves, is a duration whose elements are dissociated and juxtaposed" (MM, 186). It is a natural function of the intellect to break up the elements of duration into a succession of states or views taken from the outside. In this sense, intellectuality does grasp the real moments of duration by reconstituting them in a discontinuous series *after they are past* (CE, 200/O, 665). Western philosophy cannot accept these pragmatic forms as its own. Bergson contends that we must give up our fixation on abstract space and sympathize with the mobility of the arrow itself. By speculating on the intimate nature of mobility from within, we can restore continuity to duration and rid ourselves of the habits of spatializing time. Through this intuitive effort the contradictions of Zeno's paradox are dissolved and the passage of the arrow is revealed to be absolutely indivisible.[4]

According to Bergson, the masking of duration effected in Zeno's paradox of the arrow is repeated throughout the history of Western thought. Philosophy begins by determining the nature and function of space, defining it as an immobile medium in which objects are juxtaposed. For instance, in the *Physics*, Aristotle says that motion "in its most general and proper sense is change of place" (208a31).[5] Bergson finds that the consideration of time is always secondary to the philosophy of space. In the *Physics*, Aristotle does not engage in a systematic elaboration of time until he has established a satisfactory definition of place. "The theories of space and time . . . become counterparts of one another. To pass from one to the other, one had only to change a single word: 'juxtaposition' was replaced by 'succession'" (CM, 14/O, 14). For Bergson, time is nothing but a fourth dimension of space. Like homogeneous space, it can be carved up indefinitely and nothing changes. All of the metaphors with which time is represented are drawn from space, and all of them exclude mobility. Immanuel Kant explicates time with recourse to an analogy: "We represent the time-sequence by a line progressing to infinity, in which the manifold constitutes a series of one dimension only; and we reason from the properties of this line to all the properties of time, with this one exception, that while the parts of the line are simultaneous the parts of time are always successive" (Kant 1976, B53–58, 77).

Kant emphasizes that the parts of the line are simultaneous while the parts of the time sequence should be understood as successive. He defines time as singular, which is to say that the "parts" of time should not be understood in isolation from the whole time sequence. Nonetheless, in Bergson's terms, Kant's use of the words "succession" and "parts" are problematic because it demands that we break up time into moments placed side by side in space. Kant denies absolute reality to time. Time is nonetheless real, insofar as it is the mode of representation of myself as object (Kant 1976, B55–56, 79). It is also the mediate condition of all outer appearances because it is the *a priori* condition of all appearances whatsoever (Kant 1976, B51, 77).

For Bergson, Kant's theorization of the Transcendental Aesthetic is a compelling account of the way in which the intellect understands the relation of time and space. Bergson's objection is not so much that Kant translates time into the terms of homogeneous space, since he insists that time and space are the *a priori* forms of sensibility, but rather that Kant assumes that we are incapable of safely thinking of time and space in terms other than those dictated by the rigid frames of the understanding without lapsing into merely speculative metaphysics. In stark contrast to Kant, Bergson believes it is possible to go beyond the limits of the understanding (what Bergson calls the intellect) to obtain pure intuition (CM, 197–98/O, 1429–31). Absolute knowledge can yield thinking on time that is no longer subject to spatialization, and it can also recover concrete space, which is by no means homogeneous.

THE INTERVAL OF DURATION

Bergson asserts that the tendency to conceptualize duration as a succession of parts or instants plotted in abstract space obscures the real change unique to temporality. Duration is the uninterrupted prolongation of the past into the future. It cannot be broken up into discrete and immobile units without expelling its fundamental continuity. According to Bergson, what is counted when we symbolize time in linear terms are the "extremities of intervals" (CM, 12/O, 1254).[6] In this context, "the extremities of intervals" designate the immobile points we pick out from the line. These figures are a retrospective reconstruction of movement by the intellect. The interval (*l'intervalle*) itself is omitted from measurement because it is mobility par excellence, and mobility radically eludes calculation. Here Bergson affords the interval a particular and privileged meaning. What happens in the interval is precisely what intuition must theorize if we are to surmount the intellectual reduction of time to space (CE, 22/O, 513).

The specific meaning he reserves for "interval" stands in stark contrast to its popular use. For instance, "the interval" of a play designates a segment of clock time that marks a break in the continuity of a narrative. "Interval" in this sense is a block of homogeneous time that is readily symbolized as a line set out in space. The popular conception of the interval, then, is thoroughly consistent with the geometrical tendencies immanent to the intellectual idea of space and participates in covering up the Bergsonian interval of duration.

We cannot ask, "What is the interval of duration?" To do so would presuppose that the interval is a thing of the instantaneous present. The Bergsonian interval is rather a hyphen, a trace (*un trait d'union*) that carries the past into the future (CE, 22/O, 513). The instantaneous present is a product of abstract time and of little use to the intuitive endeavor of comprehending real duration beyond the imperatives of (Western) practice. An instant can be conceived by the intellect, but it is not perceived. Bergson writes: "When we think we have seized hold of it, it is already far away. What we actually perceive is a certain span of duration composed of two parts—our immediate past and our immediate future" (ME, 8–9/O, 818–19). The interval of duration carries the past into the future, bringing into being what did not exist. We would misunderstand Bergson if we took his description of the past and future as "two parts" of duration to mean that it can be readily divided into a pair of discontinuous units. The passage from past to future involves continuous change; the past is qualitatively different from the future that flows from it, which is why they are "two," but they remain part of an organic whole that cannot be broken up into units.

QUALITATIVE AND QUANTITATIVE DIFFERENCE

Outside of the interval in the time of the pure present, we have a discontinuous series of instants, homogeneity and spatialization. Within the interval, we find duration as a continuous, flowing qualitative alteration that is absolutely unextended. Each of these orders is characterized by its mode of differentiation, which Bergson designates respectively as quantitative and qualitative multiplicities. The difference between them is profoundly important to his philosophy as a whole and, indeed, to my own argument.

Bergson's account of the two multiplicities is developed in his first major work, *Time and Free Will*. He advances his argument through an analysis of the elementary intellectual procedure of counting and contends that the qualitative order is often obscured by and confused with spatial or quantitative multiplicity. He insists that the qualitative order has no affiliation with number (TFW, 105/O, 70). Yet, Bergson discovers that it is the condition enabling the act of counting as such.

He says that every number is at once a unity and a multiplicity of parts. Think of the number fifty. It can be conceived as a single whole or as broken up into fifty units of one. For instance, in order to count fifty sheep, we must disregard the particular qualities of each sheep. For the purpose of our calculation they are regarded as units, which are absolutely alike (TFW, 75–76/O, 51–52). In order to reach the sum of fifty, we must be able to differentiate between the sheep; otherwise, we could never conceive of more than one of them. Given that we are ignoring the qualitative distinctions between the sheep—color, size, sex, and so on—we need a way of representing them as discrete components. We are obliged to generate a homogeneous medium of space in which all of the units can be juxtaposed (TFW, 79/O, 54).

Bergson admits that the habit of counting is so familiar that we tend to dispense with the spatial diagram after the first few numbers. For example, we know twelve is half of twenty-four without resorting to imagining either figure in space. Careful analysis nonetheless reveals that every clear idea of number depends on the juxtaposition of visual images in space (TFW, 79/O, 54).

The indivisibility of each unit is symbolized by their representation as points separated by regular (spatial) intervals. Counting numbers is, according to Bergson, fundamentally discontinuous. This is because our progress from one number to the next demands that we fix our attention successively on each point. We proceed by sudden jerks (TFW, 82/O, 56). Once we have attained our total, we are inclined to join the points with a line. *After* we have performed the discontinuous calculation, we conceive the finished number as continuous. This allows us to divide up the sum indefinitely

(TFW, 83/O, 56–57). For Bergson, the fact that we can break a number up into infinitesimal parts reveals that we regard it as extended (TFW, 82/O, 56).

It is usually supposed that the operation of counting occurs in time.[7] To get to the number fifty, we repeat all the numbers we have chosen as units until we reach our desired total. Bergson writes that "the question is whether we have not counted moments of duration by means of points in space" (TFW, 78/O, 54). For each unit to be added to the next, it would have to "wait, so to speak, to be added to the others: how could it wait, if it were nothing but an instant of duration? And where could it wait if we did not localize it in space?" (TFW, 79/O, 54). If counting did occur in time and temporality was constituted by nothing but instants, we could never succeed in compounding a sum, because every component is supposed to be exactly alike. We would be condemned to counting a single unit, because we could never recognize the second unit as a different component from the first.

For Bergson, two senses of multiplicity are implied in the foregoing discussion. The units and multiplicity we conceptualize in objective space are *quantitative* determinations of number. But there is a second sense of multiplicity and unit, irreducible to the act of counting itself and purely qualitative. When we add the components of a sum aloud, we presuppose an organic totality that would alter the whole if we stopped counting at an earlier point. Take the number three as the sum we calculate by adding one plus one plus one. If we stopped after the first addition (at two) we would have a different sum. The difference between 1+1 and 1+1+1 is no doubt quantitative but, more profoundly, Bergson argues, there is a qualitative difference between the two sums. With the addition of each number in a series, a modification of the whole is effected. Every component is *internally* modified by the realization of each unit. In this sense, the numbers cannot be absolutely identical, because each one contributes its own peculiar quality to the sum. Bergson writes:

> The process by which we count units and form them into a discrete multiplicity has a double aspect; on the one hand we assume that they are identical, which is conceivable only on condition that these units are ranged alongside each other in a homogeneous medium; but on

> the other hand the third unit, for example, when added to the other two, alters the nature, the aspect and, as it were, the rhythm of the whole [*l'ensemble*]; without this mutual penetration and this, so to speak, qualitative progress, no addition would be possible. Hence it is through the quality of quantity that we form the idea of quantity without quality. [Translation modified] (TFW, 123/O, 82)

Qualitative progress is revealed as the condition of the act of counting. The units permeate one another, establishing a rhythm that enables the sum to be actualized. Their relations are not the external relations of a series of distinct components juxtaposed in space; rather, they are interpenetrating aspects in the rhythm of the whole. Without positing the unity of the whole, addition would be impossible. As Milic Capek argues, the juxtaposition of units requires not only that they are *outside* each other in space but "*together*, *beside* each other, and this togetherness resides in the *act* of juxtaposing intuition, not in its content; that is, not on the geometrical, but on the meta-geometrical level" (Capek 1971, 179). Paradoxically, the very act of positing a quantitative multiplicity bears no relation to number or extension; it is a fundamentally temporal or meta-geometrical act.

This durational process enables the spatial diagram to be materialized but cannot appear as such in the homogeneous medium it generates. Once the quantities have been set out in abstract space, the necessary function of qualitative multiplicity is obscured, because the intellect focuses on the content that is presented rather than on the act of presentation. We are thus led to consider the act of counting in purely quantitative terms. The implications of this obfuscation are tremendous for Bergson's critique of metaphysics. The relativity of knowledge is the direct result of the masking of real time with symbols set out in homogeneous space (CM, 31/O, 1272). For philosophy to become a rigorous discipline, it must differentiate between the two kinds of multiplicity: quantitative and qualitative multiplicity. If we do not acknowledge this radical distinction, we are condemned to thinking outside of duration in abstract space.

This is exactly what Bergson contends has happened in philosophy, common sense, and science. These discourses have taken account only of the spatial or quantitative order, even when they have claimed to deal with time. For instance, when we hear the sounds of a hammer striking an anvil, the blows form an indivisible whole, not unlike a melody, in which all of the notes permeate one another. Because we know the same objective cause is at work, we cut up the qualitative multiplicity into parts, which we then regard as exactly alike. This multiplicity of elements, "no longer being conceivable except by being set out in space, since they have now become identical . . . necessarily . . . [leads] to the idea of homogeneous time, the symbolical image of real duration" (TFW, 125/O, 83). But these symbols have nothing to do with the interval of duration. They are, of course, the *product* of a temporal act, but the very act of setting them out as distinct units in space jettisons the qualitative process to conceptual oblivion precisely because duration eludes representation in space.

The divergence between qualitative and quantitative multiplicities is manifest in their modes of differentiation. Let me recall Bergson's analysis of number. In this context, we must distinguish between the act of thinking number and number once it is conceived (TFW, 83/O, 57). The act of thinking it is temporal or subjective; we presuppose an organic unity in which all the units permeate one another, each contributing a specific quality to the rhythm of the whole. However, a number once thought in the medium of abstract space has become an object for the intellect. After all of the units have been set out as a series of points, or actualized by the temporal process of positing, we are powerfully inclined to join the points with the figure of a line. We then regard our sum as a continuous whole. This apparent continuity effaces the discontinuous progress of counting. Our total can then be divided indefinitely by the intellect. Number once conceived becomes an *objective* multiplicity that can be broken up in any way we please. But number in the qualitative sense cannot be divided without radically altering the aspect of the whole. Bergson thus distinguishes between the mode of differentiation effected by quantitative multiplicity and the mode of differentiation characteristic of qualitative multiplicity. Divisions within the quantitative order constitute *differences in degree*. In contrast, differentiations in the qualitative order generate radical transformations. They enact *differences in nature*.

For instance, to return to Bergson's example of a hammer striking an anvil, when the qualitative unity of the sounds perceived in intuition is projected into the homogenous time of our intellect, a profound transformation is affected. The relations between the sounds internally acting and reacting together are broken up and objectified in space. The strikes of the hammer become distinct and identical units that can be measured. This movement, from the unifying act of consciousness perceiving the sounds as a whole to their dissociation and objectification in space, is a difference in nature.

Bergsonism privileges the temporal mode of differentiation over the differences in degree generated from numerical multiplicities. Quantitative differentiation is characteristic of the intellect. It works on elements that are already given. The intellect separates, juxtaposes, and reconfigures its objects in the homogeneous medium through which it works (CM, 133/O, 1369). But its labor is focused on *what has been presented* rather than on the *act of positing* that enabled the presentation. This is manifest in Bergson's analysis of a moving object. The intellect attempts to comprehend its real change with a series of pre-given elements set out in abstract space, but these symbols do not coincide with the qualitative progress of the body's duration; they reconstruct the movement *after* it has taken place. This motionless design can serve as a useful guide to possible action but has no internal or constitutive relation to the mobility of the object.

In radical contrast, qualitative multiplicities are inventive. They precede and condition the emergence of the quantitative order but have no affiliation with number. Duration names the emergence of unforeseeable novelty that cannot be symbolized in any diagram (CM, 93). To comprehend the dynamic acts of temporal difference, philosophers must abandon the space of intellection and pursue an intuitive approach to thinking. While Bergson refuses to define intuition, he does say it has a fundamental meaning: "to think intuitively is to think in duration" (CM, 34/O, 1275). Temporal differentiation assumes *the* central role in Bergson's method; these acts characterize consciousness, the evolution of life and spirit. For Bergson, philosophy must try to follow these transformations or differences in nature. He thinks this is the only way of getting beyond the constraints imposed on thought by the demands of practical life. Bergson emphasizes that quantitative multiplicities are indispensable instruments of action.

They are incapable, however, of comprehending what happens in the interval of duration.

LANGUAGE AND THINKING

To engage in intuitive thinking is to abide with the rhythm of duration, to sympathize with its unextended mobility. Articulating a philosophy capable of thinking duration demands, of course, that Bergson makes use of language. In his view, however, purely temporal processes are different in nature from linguistic phenomena; language depends on space. We find a paradox inhering at the heart of Bergsonism: the central task of philosophy—the task of thinking time—cannot be presented in its purity (Wagner 1983, 275; Mullarkey BP, 150–51).

The reasons for this paradox, according to Bergson, derive from the origins of language, which are preeminently practical. Human beings prepare to act by setting out their movements in a homogeneous medium of space where objects can appear as distinct entities. The signs of human languages bear this intellectual tendency toward space within themselves. To be readily communicable, words and concepts require sharp and static delineations (TFW, xix/O, viii). Bergson admits that language is no longer so "blatantly [*grossièrement*] utilitarian" (CM, 80/O, 1320–21). It nonetheless continues to transmit the marks of its primary function as an instrument of action. Bergson thus defines human language as "intellectual in essence" (CM, 80/O, 1320–21). In excess of its original function, language has become more than a tool of the intellect. Poetry and literature are an example of intuition that has emerged in the course of the growth and becoming of languages. As we will see below, the fact that poetry and literature have evolved from an instrument of action are important to Bergson because they guide him toward creating a philosophical discourse that privileges the use of image and metaphor no longer harnessed to the static, intellectualized language of space so entrenched in the human heritage.

Bergson does not regard language as an instrument exclusive to the human species. Sign systems extend throughout much of the animal world. They have evolved to enable what he calls the "community of action" (CE, 157/O, 628). He believes it is likely that insect societies have a language (*langage*), which must be adapted, like our own languages, to the demands of communal life. The requirements of social life in an insect colony and those in a human society differ profoundly.[8] In insect societies there is a natural division of labor within the species such that individuals remain riveted to particular tasks (CE, 157/O, 629). The signs they exchange are likely to be restricted to the specific operations and particular objects with which they engage. This means their signs are very limited in number and *adherent* to the things and operations signified. In stark contrast, the members of a human community are capable of varying the form of their actions. Human languages must accommodate this complexity with a far greater number of signs and an ability to extend the meanings of these signs indefinitely. Unlike the instinctive sign, the intelligent sign must be *mobile* (CE, 158/O, 629).

Bergson contends that it is the mobility of the intelligent sign that has made words capable of designating not merely things but also ideas. The sophistication of the intellect is largely due, according to Bergson, to the mobility of human languages. It has extended knowledge immeasurably (CE, 158–59/O, 629–30). The problem for Western philosophy is that the intellect has not evolved to comprehend becoming, life, and duration. In order to act in the external world, the intellectual mind immobilizes. One of Bergson's central charges against the Western philosophical tradition is the consistent neglect of the fundamental law of life: the law of action. The failure to acknowledge the determining role of intellection in the evolution of knowledge has rendered metaphysics relative to the demands of human practical life. It is unsurprising to find that the conceptual logic of metaphysics is isomorphically congruent with the solid bodies that our intellect discerns from the environment. When philosophers make use of these concepts they condemn themselves to accepting the terms of a problem as it is posited by language, instead of seeking to abide with reality beyond the demands of practical life.

Bergson sometimes implies that language is an obstacle he would rather do without. In *The Creative Mind* he decries the complicity of words in the confusion between duration and space. They are "this covering we must grasp in order to tear . . . off" (*cette enveloppe qu'il faut ressaisir, pour la déchirer*) (CM, 27/O, 1269). Of course, Bergson cannot do without discourse, and he must find a way to express duration. He writes:

> The truth is that the writer's art consists above everything in making us forget that he is using words. The harmony he seeks is a certain correspondence between the comings and goings of his mind and the phrasing of his speech [*discours*], a correspondence so perfect that the waves of his thought, borne by the sentence, stir us sympathetically, and the words, taken individually, no longer count: there is nothing left but the flow of meaning [*le sens mouvant*] which runs through the words, nothing but two minds which, without intermediary, seem to vibrate directly in unison with one another.[9] (ME, 57/O, 849–50)

The best writing does not evoke our sympathy because we are affected by the materiality of sounds or marks on a page; we are stirred to thinking in unison with another mind beyond or in excess of the writing itself. He compares this experience to listening to a musician. For Bergson, music is not merely addressed to our ears. Its art, like that of great writing, is something quite other than a "material harmony of sounds." A foreigner well trained in music will not be able to distinguish between the prose we find musical and that which is not (ME, 57/O, 849). We find in Bergson's oeuvre a strong desire to exceed all symbolism and present intuition in its purity.[10]

The challenge for Bergson's philosophy is to convey the "flow of meaning" (*le sens mouvant*) without obscuring it with conventional concepts, which are saturated by spatial associations (ME, 57/O, 850). Bergson's writing employs a number of means to suggest the intuition of duration. In contrast to the dominant metaphysical tendency to value abstract discourse, he seeks forms of expression that remain "concrete" (CM, 166/O, 1399). This is why he prefers metaphors, images, and analogies to abstract conceptuality. These figures of discourse make their metaphoric, imagistic, and analogous status explicit, whereas traditional concepts efface their figural and spatial associations. A philosopher who constructs an argument made up of concepts without attending carefully to the drift of meaning necessarily implicated in the signs she or he deploys is likely to be less precise than a writer who uses metaphors with care. As he puts it in *The Creative Mind*:

> [There] are cases in which it is imagery in language [*langage*] which knowingly expresses the literal meaning [*au proper*], and abstract language which unconsciously expresses itself figuratively. The moment we reach the spiritual world, the image, if it merely seeks to suggest, may give us the direct vision, while the abstract term, which is spatial in origin and which claims to express, most frequently leaves us in metaphor. (CM, 43/O, 1285)

Paradoxically, the careful inscription of an image transcends its figurative status, while abstract discourse, unconscious of its spatial origins, tends to remain metaphorical and imagistic. For instance, in this passage Bergson's deployment of "direct vision" (*la vision directe*) suggests pure knowledge of the spiritual world (consciousness, life, memory, duration) rather than the relative knowledge of ordinary human vision. In addition to figurations of vision, he also deploys tactile and aural images to convey intuition (MM, 222/O, 355–56; CM, 147–48/O, 1383). Ironically, these images of sensation are privileged for suggesting a kind of thinking that is purely spiritual and disembodied.[11]

Bergson declares the best writing to be what evokes "our sympathy" beyond the letter of what is said. The reason poetry and literature are afforded a share of intuition is not derived from the words from which a text is constructed but from the suggestive power of a work. We must seek harmony with the intuition of a thinker in excess of what she or he has written (ME, 57/O, 849–50). When Bergson praises his contemporaries, Karin Stephen and Edouard Le Roy, each of whom published commentaries on his work, he commends them for capturing the "spirit" of his philosophy (Stephen 1922, 7; Le Roy 1913, viii). Vladimir Jankelevitch argues that to be Bergsonian we should not say what he said but make what he made; we must seek sympathy with a philosophical problem ourselves, innocently and in solitude (Jankelevitch 1959, 291). This creative effort occurs beyond discourse. In a remark about the great "masters" of philosophy, a remark that could just as well apply to his own oeuvre, Bergson contends that the philosopher could never say *what* "his" intuition was exactly, which is why "he" went on talking all "his" life. The difference between the intuition of a philosopher and the complexity of "his" doctrine, which could go on ad infinitum, is only "the incommensurability between his simple intuition and the means at his disposal for expressing it" (CM, 109/O, 1347).

In the wake of Derrida's deconstruction of the logocentric desire pervading Western philosophy, I cannot agree with Bergson's idealist separation of intuition from all forms of symbolism; thinking is material-ideal. On a related note, the fact that sensation is repeatedly invoked as a metaphor for the purity of intuition is significant. For me, Bergson's predilection for images of sensation to convey intuition's ideality betrays in negation the inextricable relation of thinking to bodily life.

DUALISM

For Bergson, dualism does not reside in a binary opposition between a concept and its other floundering in untheorized confusion but between two divergent modes of differentiation. He believes space divides only by degree, while duration generates differences in nature. Qualitative differentiations are not merely reconfigurations of preexisting elements; they are necessarily creative acts.

On his argument, the emergence of space is the result of a purely temporal differentiation. Paradoxically, the temporal nature of difference is obscured from human beings by the tendency toward space immanent to the mind. He believes this tendency toward space is the mainspring of the human intellect, the form of knowledge that evolved to aid human action in the world.

I have argued that Bergson's thesis on the intellect as the form of practical human knowledge is ethnocentric. Bergson's thesis is possible because he has homogenized "human being" with insufficient regard for the evolution of divergent systems of thought and life among peoples. In Australia, there are Aboriginal ontologies in which the logic of quantification, homogeneity, and measurement do not operate. "We are not merely on and in the land, we are of it, we speak as one voice of the Creation, the voice or song law. Land and people are one voice, one song" (Watson 2002, 7).[12]

Even though Bergson's critique of spatialization and quantification does not have universal applicability, it is valuable for assessing the evolution of Western thought and for rethinking duration. I sympathize with Bergson's polemic against the logic of quantification and measurement, a logic bequeathed by Western intellection, though my own position takes some distance from his dualism. I have contested Bergson's hierarchical presentation of the relation between thought and language. The following chapters suggest this is a sexed hierarchy, in which thought (duration, life, and consciousness) is valorized over language (space, matter). While I support Bergson's struggle against homogeneity and quantification, I argue that his durational philosophy is more indebted to spatiality and materiality than he admits. Perhaps it is possible to affirm materiality and spatiality without falling into a homogenizing logic of pure space and pure quantification?

5. Interval, Sexual Difference

I do not intend . . . to enter upon a comparative study of the two sexes. Suffice it to say that woman is as intelligent as man, but that she is less capable of emotion, and that if there is any faculty or power [*puissance*] of the soul which seems to attain less development in woman than in man, it is not intelligence, but sensibility. I mean of course sensibility in the depths [*la sensibilité profonde*], not agitation at the surface.

BERGSON 1977, 44/O, 1012

THIS CHAPTER OFFERS a feminist critique of the primary intuition of Henri Bergson's philosophy, his celebrated deduction of consciousness as duration (CM, 12–14/O, 1254–56). I suggest that his intuition of the enduring self is elaborated within paternal parameters. This claim is not intended as a condemnation of Bergson's thinking in the name of feminist theory. On the contrary, I want to consider how we may reread his intuition of the enduring self in relation to Luce Irigaray's formulation of the interval of sexual difference.

In Irigaray's work, sexual difference has at least two senses. First, "sexual difference" is a critical description of the violent sexed hierarchy that covertly inaugurates metaphysics as phallocentrism. Second, "sexual difference" is the opening to thought and to life, which figures man and woman in a nonhierarchical relationship (ESD/E).

Hierarchical sexual difference elevates the conceptual architecture of philosophy by positing a disavowed outside. Irigaray emphasizes that the stakes of this violent relation are sexed; metaphysics articulates concepts that are isomorphically congruent with the male sex and excludes what she calls "the maternal-feminine." For Irigaray, the maternal-feminine is the unthematizable material foundation cast outside of metaphysics in order for metaphysics to function. In this sense, sexual difference inaugurates philosophy but is construed as a violent hierarchy.

Irigaray's project goes beyond *describing* the sexed hierarchy underwriting metaphysics, to posit a new formulation of sexual difference. Her radical proposal situates man and woman in a horizontal relation that is irreducible. In stark contrast to the phallocentric figuration of philosophy, Irigaray proposes that the masculine and feminine poles of life should be reconceived as autonomous thresholds of becoming. The maternal-feminine would no longer function as the repressed ground of knowledge, because thought would begin from the sexuate *relation* or *interval* between man and woman. These sexed poles of life would not be given as static concepts; they would be constituted through the differentiating movement of the interval (ESD, 48–49/E, 53–54). In this formulation, thinking is no longer understood as a neutral activity: thinking is articulated through the interval as a sexuate relation.

The privilege that Irigaray confers on the interval of sexual difference in its radical sense—*the* difference from which thinking emerges—has important implications for her critique of the monosexual economy of conventional metaphysics. Where radical sexual difference foregrounds the interval between man and woman as the opening of thought, philosophy traditionally proceeds from an obscurity. The inaugural act of differentiation enabling metaphysics to separate itself from the maternal-feminine is unthought within metaphysics. In other words, in the philosophical tradition, both the maternal-feminine and the interval flounder together in obscurity (IR, 169/ESD, 10/E, 17–18).

The interval is fundamental to Irigaray's project. In nonhierarchical sexual difference, the interval is posited as the opening of thinking and life, while in the monosexual economy of metaphysics the interval is the secret lever of differentiation that buries the material-feminine and elevates philosophy as phallocentrism.

To my knowledge, Irigaray does not engage with Bergson's philosophy specifically. Yet, as Dorothea Olkowski and Elizabeth Grosz have pointed out, there are significant affinities between Irigaray's and Bergson's respective projects (Olkowski RR, 80–83; BI; Grosz NT, 14). I suggest that Bergson's thinking on duration is, in some ways, remarkably resonant with Irigaray's figuration of the interval of sexual difference. Bergson privileges a concept of the interval as the opening of time, or what he calls duration (*la durée*). The interval of duration is nothing other than the threshold of intuition, the method he believes philosophy must pursue in order to become a rigorous form of knowledge. The Bergsonian interval is not subordinate to identity or calculability. On the contrary, his interval is the threshold of difference, the condition of possibility of identity, matter, and space that exceeds all attempts at calculation and prediction.

Like Irigaray, Bergson ascribes fundamental importance to a formulation of the interval as the opening of thinking and life from which space and time might be reconceived. In contrast to Olkowski and Grosz, I do not contend that this striking resonance between them should be construed as a claim that Irigaray's conception of the interval is directly compatible with Bergson's interval and his method of intuition (Olkowski RR, 80–83; BI; Grosz NT, 14).[1] On the contrary, I argue that Bergson's contention that space and matter are products of the interval of duration is imbricated in the repression of the maternal-feminine and in the elevation of a paternal concept of consciousness. For Irigaray, the interval is sexed and must be conceived as both spatial *and* temporal and material *and* transcendental.

In spite of the sexed hierarchy that organizes his project, Bergson has a lot to offer Irigaray scholarship. Irigaray's writing on the temporality of the interval is dense and aphoristic. In this context, Bergson's painstaking elaboration of the reasons why duration must remain beyond the strictures of conventional definition is valuable for making sense of Irigaray's account of the interval. If Bergson's theorization of duration is helpful for thinking the Irigarayan interval of sexual difference, Irigaray's philosophy is indispensable for a feminist reading of Bergson. Irigaray provides a framework for diagnosing the hierarchically sexed assumptions of Bergson's project and also for a transvaluation of his thinking. To read Bergson with Irigaray is to affirm the inextricability of spatiality and corporeality from the interval of duration.

CONSCIOUSNESS AS DURATION

As Roland Breeur notes, Bergson's deduction of consciousness as duration begins negatively. In order to obtain an intuition of the enduring self, all forms of spatial symbolism must be put out of play (BR 2001, 180). Homogeneous space is the medium of the intellect, and intellection is indispensable to science and to the demands of practical life. The problem, for Bergson, is that homogeneous space has become such a habitual form of human knowledge that the metaphysical tradition has failed to notice how it masks the flow of real time. Space is the medium into which time is contorted. The disfiguring influence of space is perhaps most pronounced in the intellectual description of consciousness. Psychic life is figured as a succession of states. When psychic life is presented as a succession of states, change would seem to reside in the passage from one state to another. For Bergson, change is far more radical than the intellect can admit. He insists that the self is nothing but change; it consists of a continuous passage or flow of duration (CE, 1–2/O, 495).

To conceive of the self as a succession of discontinuous states is to break up consciousness into a powder of equivalent moments that are readily reducible to number. As Bergson emphasizes, number cannot account for the continuously evolving quality of the self's duration. In order to identify the succession of states as a particular consciousness, this quantitative multiplicity must be posited as a unity. The intellectual thinker is thus compelled to construct a "formless ego" (*un* moi *amorphe*), which holds all of the states of consciousness together (CE, 3–4/O, 497).

For Bergson, there is no "formless" spatial ego, and consciousness does not consist of a collection of states. Instead, he argues, the inner life of the self is an uninterrupted flow of duration. The continuity of consciousness as duration must also be understood as heterogeneous. The word "heterogeneous" should not be read in spatial terms. It refers to the qualitative alteration of enduring consciousness in relation to itself. According to Bergson, the heterogeneity of the self as duration has no affiliation with number or space. It is an evolving whole whose aspects do not externalize themselves. It is purely qualitative (TFW, 104/O, 69).

Bergson's conceptualization of the enduring self as a flow of interpenetrating elements seeks to foreground the very passage of duration. He presents the duration of consciousness as the hyphen, or connecting link, that brings the past into the future (CE, 22/O, 513). In short, he conceives of enduring consciousness as the threshold of emergence that brings into being what did not exist. In *Time and Free Will*, the self as duration is celebrated as the very condition of qualitative difference. This temporal interval is the threshold of invention that introduces free acts into the world. Even the act of generating a medium of homogeneous space is a temporal act. Space, for Bergson, is dependent on the interval of duration in order to exist.

THE ENDURING SELF AND SPACE

There is a paradox at work in the deduction of the enduring self, which Bergson does not analyze. The intuition of consciousness as duration depends profoundly on what Bergson would call an intellectual conception of the self.[2] In order to identify "our own person in its flowing through time," Bergson must maintain a distinction between the inner life of the self and its outside (CM, 162/O, 1396). This distinction between the inside and the outside of the self is spatial. Despite his stated intentions in *Time in Free Will*, Bergson is unable to sustain a sharp separation between duration and space (TFW, 229/O, 149).

We know that Bergson ascribes a secondary status to space and its acts of differentiation. They are the products of the temporal interval, which emerge from the enduring self. However, because Bergson relies on the instituting difference between self and other, the primacy he attributes to his conception of the temporal interval cannot be maintained. Bergsonian qualitative difference is haunted by an act of division, which, within the terms of his project, is a spatial division. In the context of deducing the durational self, this corporeal difference cannot be a mere practical exigency, nor can it be purely spatial; it is irreducible to the identification of a particular enduring consciousness and its specific temporal acts. In Irigarayan terms, this act of differentiation is the constitutive gesture of philosophy that effects a violent sexed hierarchy by casting the maternal-feminine as the material ground on which thought is erected. I contend that Bergson's intuition of the enduring self is yet another manifestation of a sexed hierarchy.

Irigaray understands the maternal-feminine as the unacknowledged substratum on which philosophy depends in order to be posited. The maternal-feminine functions as the place of philosophy without ever constituting a place for herself. She has no identity except as the undifferentiated matter from which metaphysics distinguishes itself as pure speculation. Her role as the necessary substratum of thought cannot be acknowledged within philosophy, because metaphysics depends on her repression in order to function. Yet, Irigaray argues, this founding act of obfuscation leaves traces within philosophy. On the one hand, the privileged articulations of metaphysics are unconsciously congruent with phallic masculinity and, on the other hand, anything within philosophical discourse that threatens to recall the maternal-feminine is denigrated. In this sense, philosophy repeats within its own system the founding violence of its conception. While Irigaray does not address Bergson's oeuvre in her writing, I believe that her argument is confirmed when we pay careful attention to the silenced condition enabling the discovery of enduring consciousness. His conception of the self is posited in apparent ignorance of the primary material (or maternal) conditions from which it springs. However, as we will see, his own text acts out a sexed hierarchy in the figuration of the relation between the enduring self and the "parasitic" spatial self (TFW, 166/O, 110).

Bergson's understanding of materiality is not directly related to a phallocentric figuration of the female sex in *Time and Free Will*, but there is no question that it is denigrated at the expense of pure duration. Matter and homogeneous space are denounced for disfiguring the comprehension of consciousness. The intellect projects the self into homogeneous space because it models its procedures on matter. He insists that philosophy must go beyond this "parasitic" self in order to abide with the pure quality of fundamental consciousness. The spatialized self is merely secondary, a product of the demands of human action, which obscures the novelty of duration. In my view, the very act of privileging the enduring self as the genuine version of consciousness betrays a hierarchy of the masculine and the feminine. The sexuate status of this theoretical imperative is rendered explicit when Bergson uses the metaphor of paternity to describe the relationship between the enduring self and the free acts the self engenders. Matter, conversely, is rendered feminine by implication, at least in *Time and Free Will*. The feminine status of matter is more marked in Bergson's work on evolution. For example, he claims in *Creative Evolution* that matter approaches "absolute passivity" and, in *Mind-Energy*, that matter in the hands of "Man" is forced into the status of a mere "instrument" (CE, 200/O, 665; ME, 26/O, 830).

Because Bergson presents matter and space as a projection that deforms the qualitative duration of the self, femininity would seem to lurk within spatialized consciousness. This might appear odd, given that Irigaray (among others) has argued that philosophy has always defined consciousness as masculine.[3] However, Bergsonian spatialized consciousness is not true consciousness. It is a mere construct that obliterates the genuine articulations of thought. The spatial self is merely the product of the temporal self; it is not credited with the ability to create. I contend that the degraded status of this version of the self—as spatial, as secondary, as a mere construct that is modeled on matter—is a trace of its femininity. In this context, femininity is a determined concept mastered by the masculine procedures of the philosopher: it is phallocratic femininity.

Bergson's durational consciousness is implicitly entangled in corporeality and a certain (nonhomogeneous) order of spatiality. But this corporeal specter lurking within the enduring self is not acknowledged by Bergson, and this enables him to explicitly devalue matter and space without appearing to compromise his privileged version of consciousness. Homogeneous space, or what I am calling "phallocratic femininity," functions as the bearer of matter and space for the supposedly disembodied *durée* of the self.

Irigaray argues that the conceptual heritage of metaphysics has maintained a complicity of long standing with solid bodies (TS, 107/CS, 106). She identifies an isomorphic congruence between the solidity of philosophical concepts and phallic masculinity and, at the same time, she contends that metaphysics exhibits repulsion toward fluidity. Irigaray suggests also that this abhorrence is analogous to the horror of the female sex (IR, 64/SA, 294–95). The fluid, like woman, is what exceeds presentation within philosophical discourse. She-it disconcerts the ordered systematicity of phallocentric metaphysics.

Bergson is decidedly unconventional in this context. In his corpus, solids are devalued at the expense of the pure fluidity of duration, and, like Irigaray, he is critical of logic as preeminently the logic of solids. For Bergson, the main reason metaphysics has privileged solids is entangled in the intellect's preoccupation with inert bodies. Concepts have been modeled on matter because philosophy has remained the unwitting prisoner of the laws of practical life. In order to theorize duration, solid logic must be abandoned, and he proposes that the flow of consciousness should be understood as fluidity itself (CE, ix–x, xii–iii; 46/O, 489–490, 492, 534).

While Bergson's valorization of fluidity is not conventionally phallocentric, it would be precipitous to assimilate his reversal of the fluid–solid hierarchy to a revaluation of the feminine in relation to the traditional privilege ascribed to the solid forms of metaphysics. He celebrates fluids as a more promising means to suggest duration, while solids are construed as a blockage to the recovery of true temporality. According to the terms presented by Bergson's discourse, a sexed hierarchy operates between the fluidity of paternal duration and the solid determinism of feminine matter.

For Bergson, the feminine space of the secondary self is the material obstacle to the discovery of fundamental consciousness. She-it is figured as other to the duration of psychic life. In Irigarayan terms, this phallocratic version of femininity is not the other of consciousness, because she is allowed no alterity. Her-its being is presumed to be entirely determined under the philosopher's gaze and as homogeneous space. She can be divided and measured. In the works subsequent to *Time and Free Will*, Bergson concedes that solidity is a form that the intellect projects onto matter rather than a determined state of it (1981, 199). Feminized matter in his later work is not purely calculable. But even when feminine matter is not presented as coincident with homogeneous space and the calculations of the intellect, she-it threatens Bergson's argument, because it is in considering her-it that we realize that durational consciousness is far more dependent on matter than Bergson acknowledges. She-it threatens to recall the embodiment of paternal consciousness and the material outside from which he was born: the maternal-feminine. In this context, the denigration of the feminine space of the secondary self becomes necessary to shore up the paternal privilege of consciousness as duration.

The radical alterity of the maternal-feminine is not reducible to phallocratic femininity. The maternal-feminine cannot be presented within the discourse of philosophy. In Bergson's text, she-it is the secret outside to the repressed corporeality of the enduring self. Her-its constitutive role can be discerned only as a trace within the concept of phallocratic femininity. We find that phallocratic femininity obscures the inaugural acts of Bergson's philosophical experiment. Her-its position as the material obstacle to the enduring self covers over the corporeality of man's consciousness and the maternal-feminine ground from which he covertly differentiates himself. This unacknowledged act of differentiation is nothing other than the interval of sexual difference acting to effect a violent hierarchization.

While the devalued femininity of matter remains implicit in Bergson's first major work, durational consciousness is sexed. The sexualization of the enduring self occurs when Bergson defends the primary thesis of *Time and Free Will*: the human capacity to introduce a free act into the world. The genesis of this act is nothing other than the temporal interval. He writes: "In a word, if it is agreed to call every act free which springs from the self and from the self alone, the act which bears the mark of our personality is truly free, for our self alone will lay claim to its paternity" (TFW, 173/O, 114).[4]

The Bergsonian self is posited as the father of the free act. In keeping with his formulation, we could say that the purely qualitative difference of the interval is the seminal expression of the paternal personality. Indeed, the paternal genesis of free acts is precisely what defines fundamental consciousness as duration.

Some philosophers might object that this paternal scenario is merely metaphorical. Aristotle, for instance, was wary of metaphor (97b31–39). However, Bergson believes that a rigorously deployed metaphor is a highly effective means to convey duration. A metaphor cannot present an intuition, because language is spatial, yet metaphor can suggest the intuition of duration in a "direct vision" (CM, 43/O, 1285). Bergson's use of the metaphor of paternity is not meant literally. Yet the father's creation of his child—the insemination of the unacknowledged matter of the egg—is suggestive of the relationship between the enduring self and the act the self engenders.

According to Bergson's depiction in *Time and Free Will* of the paternal genesis of the free act, woman is implicitly denied the capacity to engender free acts. Or, insofar as she is capable of articulating a free act, she does not do so *as a woman*. I make this claim partly on the basis of a passage from Bergson's later work. His depiction of the paternal genesis of the free act in *Time and Free Will* is remarkably consistent with this passage from his last major study, *The Two Sources of Morality and Religion*.

> I do not intend . . . to enter upon a comparative study of the two sexes. Suffice it to say that woman is as intelligent as man, but that she is less capable of emotion, and that if there is any faculty or power [*puissance*] of the soul which seems to attain less development in woman than in man, it is not intelligence, but sensibility. I mean of course sensibility in the depths [*la sensibilité profonde*], not agitation at the surface. (1977, 44/O, 101)

Bergson declares that woman is generally less capable of "deep sensibility" than man. Here, "deep sensibility" refers to intuition, and the articulation of free acts is constitutive of intuition. In a footnote, he goes on to explain that the reason "deep sensibility" attains less development in woman than in man is probably ordained by nature.[5] The best of her supra-intellectual capacities are restricted to motherhood. Bergson does qualify his contention that woman is less capable of intuition than man by admitting that there are "many exceptions." As I read him, exceptional women who develop deep sensibility do so in spite of their sex (1977, 44–45/O, 1012).

If in Bergson's first major work woman is implicitly denied the power of generating a free act, in his last book she is explicitly judged as less capable of articulating the free acts of intuition. For Bergson, the genesis of free acts is framed within paternal parameters.

The invocation of a paternal metaphor to describe the enduring self's capacity to articulate free acts should also be read as a trace of sexed corporeal difference. On the one hand, Bergson's argument specifically expels feminine matter and space in order to obtain an intuition of duration, and, on the other hand, he brings embodiment back into the thought experiment by conferring a sexuate status on enduring consciousness. The irreducible act of sexual differentiation between self and other is played out in the metaphor of paternity. This metaphor betrays the sexed hierarchy on which the deduction of durational consciousness is erected. The maternal-feminine is the silenced other of the embodied paternal self. Without unconsciously placing her there, beyond the focus of his intuition, Bergson could not identify consciousness as such.[6]

If the maternal-feminine is acknowledged as the ground of the intuition of duration, she can no longer remain as ground, and the self can no longer be posited as purely qualitative duration. This amounts to threatening the very foundation of duration's priority over matter and space. The privilege conferred on paternal duration is called into question because its progress is revealed as radically dependent on the maternal-feminine in order to articulate itself. In this context, Bergson's presentation of a hierarchical relation between pure duration and spatiality—or between Man and the phallocratic version of the feminine—begins to unravel. Man can know his duration only as his, thanks to his own sexed body. He does not discover himself in a solipsistic act of identification with the pure flow of his person in time; his embodied duration is revealed in relation to the alterity of the maternal-feminine. In Irigarayan terms, the differentiation between man and the maternal-feminine is the interval of sexual difference acting to establish a violent hierarchy. We find it is not only the maternal-feminine that flounders in theoretical obscurity. The interval of sexual difference is also occluded by Bergson's intuitive approach to duration.

My critique of Bergson renders his deduction of enduring consciousness and the interval of duration problematic. It suggests that the temporal interval and his conception of the self as duration are framed within paternal parameters that exclude feminine subjectivity. I have also argued that his relegation of space to a secondary status posterior to the qualitative differentiations of the temporal interval does not hold up. A disavowed spatial and corporeal differentiation is required to establish the paternal self as pure quality. Acknowledging these repressed conditions in Bergson's thinking does not amount to a rejection of his groundbreaking work on the specific dynamics of duration. On the contrary, I think his work remains valuable for thinking through Irigaray's highly aphoristic account of the interval of sexual difference.

INTERVAL, SEXUAL DIFFERENCE

Like Bergson, Irigaray develops a formulation of the interval as the opening to thought and to life. Where Bergson's interval is discovered in relation to a solitary and disembodied consciousness, Irigaray's interval is posited in direct relation to the corporeality of sexed subjects. This is explicit in her work. The interval of sexual difference is incarnated in the actual relationship between the bodies of woman and man *here and now*. Yet this present relation is paradoxical, for the interval always remains in play as an excessive locus to the past and the future. In this context, she emphasizes that the interval resists definition (IR 167–68, 172; 176/E, 15; 20; 25).

Irigaray's insistence upon the excessiveness of the interval is crucial to safeguarding "its" status as the threshold of temporality that cannot be subjected to calculation and homogeneous space. Why are calculation and homogeneous space so problematic? Bergson's thinking on duration is instructive here. As he demonstrates, calculability presupposes a medium of homogeneous space and homogeneous space pulverizes the qualitative change of the interval's duration into a powder of equivalent moments that are readily reducible to number. In other words, number cannot symbolize the evolving quality of the interval nor can number account for the interval's openness (Bergson TFW, 79/O, 54). For Irigaray and Bergson, the interval must be conceived as the threshold to the future and to the past. The future is, in principle, unforeseeable, while the being of the past always remains in excess of recuperation in the present (Irigaray IR, 167–68, 175, 176/E, 16; 24; 25; Bergson CM, 35/O, 1275; MM, 168–69/O, 307–8). To sympathize with the becoming of the interval we must resist imagining the interval as a calculable relation in homogeneous space.

Bergson believes it is necessary to retreat from corporeality and spatiality as such in order to overcome the obfuscation of the temporality of the interval by homogeneous space. Irigaray's repeated emphasis upon the undefinability of the interval demonstrates that she shares Bergson's aversion to homogeneous space, but she does not seek to abandon spatiality per se. The order of spatiality at work in her formulation of the interval is heterogeneous and irreducible to presence.

My critical description of Bergson shows that his claim to overcome space fails. His deduction of the interval is predicated upon the irreducibly extensive limit between a living body and "its" outside. The discovery of duration is achieved through the subject's encounter with the alterity of the duration of the sexed other. Acknowledging this transcendence inscribes the very limits of the self.

For Irigaray, the acknowledgement of a subject's limits does not foreclose knowledge but serves as a threshold to the articulation of sexed intersubjectivity. She invites her readers to imagine a subject in the passage of her becoming who remains open to the unassimilable duration of the sexed other (ESD, 112/E, 109). The subject's openness is not something that emerges from her becoming, for this opening, the interval of sexual difference, is the very possibility of her becoming. The interval is not outside of her; the interval acts at the threshold of her body, giving her a limit that is her sexuate identity and also a passage toward the becoming of an other subject, man. For Irigaray this passage between woman and man is nothing other than the opening of thought and life. Each sex is constituted through the interval and thought is no longer a solipsistic inquiry conducted by a lone subject, it is reconceived as collaborative work articulated by both sexes. The interval is not given once and for all; the interval always remains in play, exceeding the sensible relation between woman and man as the very possibility of sexual difference (ESD, 49, 147/E, 54, 139).

The fundamental task of Irigaray's oeuvre is to think and live the difference between the human sexes nonhierarchically. And yet the nature of her construal of difference remains open, in principle, to the generation of other kinds of relations.

The following chapter returns to Bergson and evaluates the monistic turn elaborated in his work after *Time and Free Will*. His thinking on monism is a sustained effort to think difference beyond the human as the very motor of life, of becoming. I believe this direction in his thought is promising for taking feminist thinking on difference beyond an anthropocentric terrain.

6. Beyond Man: Rethinking Life and Matter

> Philosophy should be an effort to go beyond
> the human condition.
>
> BERGSON

> We always get back to this definition: the machinic
> phylum is materiality, natural or artificial,
> and both simultaneously; it is matter in
> movement, in flux, in variation,
> matter as conveyor of
> singularities and traits of expression.
>
> DELEUZE AND GUATTARI 1987, 409

BERGSON IS IMPORTANT precisely because of his sustained effort to think difference beyond subject and object, as becoming, as the very force of life. Chapter Six evaluates his postulation of a posthuman thinking of life as difference for traces of humanism and phallocentrism.[1] This judgmental approach is not proposed in order to shut Bergson down. I want to emphasize the strands of his thinking of difference I love, strands that may enable a posthuman philosophy of sexual difference. But I do not believe this can be achieved without a critique of the misogyny at work in his project.

Sometimes he presents the concept of life in opposition to matter. At other times matter and life are found together. This is not a contradiction; Bergsonism is both a dualistic and a monistic metaphysics. Deleuze argues that Bergson's use of dualism is methodological. He dichotomizes in order to recover duration from the solid forms of homogeneous space (Deleuze B, 29/BE, 20). After distinguishing living phenomena from space, Bergson reintegrates life and matter into an evolving whole in which the difference between the creative speeds of life and the almost determined rhythm of matter is a difference in temporal tension (Deleuze B, 29/BE, 20). I have argued that his use of dualism is more than methodological and indicates a sexed hierarchy at the heart of his project. This chapter suggests that the impact of Bergson's phallocentrism goes beyond his formulation of the duration of human consciousness to structure the purportedly transhuman study of the life–matter relation. Further, I suggest that his celebrated monistic integration of the divergent tendencies of life and matter maintains this sexed hierarchy.

There are excesses at work in Bergson's thinking of life as difference that overflow the dominant configuration of the life–matter relation as phallocentrism. These excesses are significant resources in the struggle to exceed the human and to escape phallocentrism. To emphasize these aspects of his thinking is also to transform Bergson or, more precisely, to transform the dominant configurations in his project of the relationships between matter and life, extensity and duration, passivity and activity, and the feminine and the masculine.

After *Time and Free Will*, Bergson radicalizes his conception of consciousness to propose that consciousness is characteristic of life. This maneuver is crucial to his antihumanism. I argue that it is also, paradoxically, the gesture that carries phallic-anthropomorphism into his effort to articulate a philosophy of life outside the human condition. His remarkable account of consciousness is the subject of the next section. Subsequent sections detail the extent to which a disavowed sexed hierarchy organizes Bergson's postulation of a posthuman consciousness–matter relation. This critique is offered as a way into making use of Bergson as a thinker of difference as life but without reiterating his phallocentrism. Drawing on Manuel de Landa, Deleuze, Grosz, and Irigaray, I hope to show how Bergson can be read as a thinker of nonhierarchical sexual difference and difference. The conclusion of this chapter rewrites Bergsonian difference as an extensive and intensive, passive and active becoming outside the order of number.

CONSCIOUSNESS AS TENDENCY

In *Matter and Memory*, consciousness is presented as a practical faculty that emerges when an individual is confronted by a challenge in its environment. Consciousness is a spatial and temporal hesitation that enables the living being to draw on memory in order to select an appropriate response to its current situation (MM, 32, 141/O, 183, 283; ME, 13–14/O, 821–22). In some beautiful pages in the Huxley lecture, Bergson suggests that consciousness is by no means peculiar to humans or even to animals with brains. While animals with brains have a greater power of deliberation and possible action than those without them, even a simple protoplasmic mass has a "confused" order of consciousness to call on in order to prepare to act in its world. He proposes that consciousness is "in principle co-extensive with life." Plants, for example, are characterized by a dormant form of consciousness rather than an absence of it (ME, 11–16/O, 820–24).

Bergson's concept of consciousness is not a static, ever-present faculty in the living being. Conscious deliberation is precisely an oscillation and a reflection on the possible actions to be undertaken by an individual. It emerges when the living being is unsure how to act in its world, and it departs when the organism is engaged in habitual activity that does not require deliberation. For example, an infant learning to walk—stumbling, lurching forward for a few clumsy steps, and falling over—must consciously reflect on his activity, because he has not yet trained his body to enact these movements without the intervention of consciousness. In contrast, when a woman is engaged in a habitual activity such as swimming laps in a pool she knows well, her movements and orientation are automatic. In Bergson's terms, the action of swimming is unconscious. While consciousness is the very threshold of the potentiality for freedom in a living being, this potentiality for freedom emerges only when an organism needs to deliberate over its action.

Bergson gives another slant to his conceptualization of consciousness in *The Creative Evolution*. Consciousness is figured as a pre-individual force in the becoming of life. It is an evolving tendency actualizing "itself" in different species over millennia. This maneuver is particularly important, because it presents consciousness as a differential force that articulates different forms but is not exhausted in its instantiations in particular beings. To figure consciousness in these terms is to attempt to exceed the strictures of the (human) subject and the incarnation of consciousness in relation a particular living being. Yet there is a significant problem with Bergson's figuration of consciousness as tendency. Consciousness is a force of ascent that names the very activity of life that is opposed to the descent and passivity of matter. As we will see, it is nothing other than the masculine half of Bergson's sexed hierarchy.

THE FORCE OF ASCENT AND THE FORCE OF DESCENT

In *The Creative Evolution*, Bergson traces a line of demarcation between matter and the living (CE 197–8/O, 663). Within the whole, each inclines in the opposite direction: the movement of the inert is one of descent, whereas consciousness is a movement of ascent. Materiality adds nothing new to the whole from moment to moment, and, in principle, its pulsations "might be accomplished almost instantaneously, like releasing a spring." It merely unwinds a roll ready prepared. In contrast, the ascending movement of life "corresponds to an inner work of ripening or creating." Becoming is life. It "*endures* essentially, and imposes its rhythm on the first [matter], which is inseparable from it" (CE, 11/O, 503).

Bergson affirms repeatedly that, insofar as inert matter is bound up in the duration of the universe, it endures. "The universe *endures*. . . . The systems marked off by science *endure* only because they are bound up inseparably with the rest of the universe" (CE, 11/O, 503). He provides what is now a famous example to support his argument. If sugar is mixed in a glass of water, the observer cannot speed up or draw out the process of the sugar melting. The observer's impatience is not something thought, such as the mathematical time of the physicist; it corresponds to something lived. Waiting for the sugar to melt is not relative, because the parts of time cannot be unfurled at will. It is absolute. The whole universe has a particular, irreducible rhythm of duration that is something like a consciousness (CE, 10/O, 502). In other words, matter is irreducibly implicated in the duration of the living.

Intuition provides Bergson with the means to elucidate the relationship between life and matter. Characteristically, he calls for the philosopher to reflect on "his" own interior life. In his view, this act of thinking introduces the philosopher to an intuition of the two contrary movements that make up the Whole, the movement of life and the movement of matter. To accomplish the movement of life, "we" must seek, within "our own" experience, "the point where we feel ourselves most intimately with our own life. It is into pure duration that we then plunge back; a duration in which the past, always moving on, is swelling unceasingly with a present that is absolutely new" (translation modified; CE, 199–200/O, 664–65). This effort is strenuous because it goes against the ingrained human habit of spatializing time. While this is an act of reflection on the "inner life," the temporal rhythm that the philosopher strives to discover here is not the duration of "his" own life but the duration of life itself. Bergson emphasizes that the intuitive thinker can never reach this limit of pure duration, which is nothing other than freedom itself.[2]

Materiality tends in the opposite direction. From the effort of contracting as much as possible of "our" past into the present in an undivided continuity, Bergson invites "us" to dilate our consciousness, as far as possible.

> If the relaxation [*détente*] were complete, there would no longer be either memory or will—which amounts to saying that, in fact, we never do fall into this absolute passivity, any more than we can make ourselves absolutely free. But, in the limit, we get a glimpse [*nous entrevoyons*] of an existence made of a present which recommences unceasingly—devoid of real duration, nothing but the instantaneous which dies and is born again endlessly. (CE, 200–1/O, 665)

Materiality *inclines* in the direction of absolute passivity but never fully dilates. If it did, it would become pure space.[3] As Bergson concedes, "analysis resolves it into elementary vibrations, the shortest of which are of very slight duration, almost vanishing, but not nothing" (CE, 201/O, 665). Matter and life are thus defined as two opposing tendencies: the ascending movement approaching creation and freedom, and the descending movement inclining toward pure repetition. In this context Bergson is able say that matter is the interruption of duration

(CE, 201/O, 665–66). Given that the entire universe endures and that materiality is irreducibly bound up in all aspects of the whole, this interruption occurs within duration, although it inclines in the inverse direction to the one articulated in the becoming of life.

For Bergson, the double effort of contraction and dilation in consciousness proceeds from the plane of experience but incites the philosopher beyond it, toward the purely qualitative and purely quantitative. Intuition is really a traversal between two extremes: unextended qualitative duration, which is absolutely continuous, and extended quantitative repetition, which lends itself to calculation and division. For Bergson

> the intuition of duration . . . brings us into contact with a whole continuity of durations which we should try to follow, either downwardly or upwardly: in both cases we can dilate ourselves indefinitely by a more and more vigorous [*violent*] effort, in both cases we transcend ourselves. In the first, we advance towards a duration more and more scattered [*éparpillée*], whose palpitations, more rapid than ours, dividing our simple sensation, dilute its quality into quantity: at the limit would be the pure homogeneous, the pure repetition by which we define materiality. In advancing in the other direction, we go toward a duration which stretches, tightens, and becomes more and more intensified: at the limit would be eternity. This time not only conceptual eternity, which is an eternity of death, but an eternity of life. It would be a living, and consequently still moving eternity, where our duration would find itself like the vibrations in light, and which would be the concentration of all duration, as materiality is its dispersion [*l'éparpillement*]. Between these two extreme limits moves intuition, and this movement is metaphysics itself. (CM, 187–8/O, 1419)

We can see from the vertical movement of intuition described in this passage how Bergson reconciles the dualisms. Between the extremes of freedom and necessity, there are so many different degrees of tension, so many different degrees of extension.[4]

Bergson's temporal monism plainly privileges life over matter. On the one hand, life is celebrated for approaching freedom, and, on the other hand, matter tends toward necessity. Where life has the dynamic capacity to draw on the virtual and engender new configurations in the actual, matter is confined to the plane of the present, in which it ceaselessly makes itself from moment to moment. This hierarchical relationship is not explicitly sexed. Nonetheless, Bergson deploys traditionally phallocentric images to describe life and matter. Matter is associated with "absolute passivity," an expression with well-known feminine connotations in the misogynist sense (MM, 200/O, 665). In contrast, life is presented in heroically masculine terms as a movement of ascent approaching freedom. It is not just Bergson's use of metaphor that is sexed; the very structure of the spatial relations that Bergson deploys in his image of duration as a monism has phallic connotations. Pure duration is at the summit of the Whole, while matter serves as the base.

SEMINAL CREATIVITY

The sexed hierarchy in Bergson's formulation of the relationship between life and matter is perhaps most pronounced in his account of evolution. Paradoxically, the emergence of sexual generation as such receives scant attention in his description of evolution's dynamic progress.

Bergson posits the *élan vital* as a virtual multiplicity, which in its initial impulsion held an immense reservoir of forces within itself. These forces contained mutually antagonistic aspects. In order to allow them an ability to grow, the forces were obliged to split up into distinct tendencies. We have arrived at one of the central theses of Bergson's most famous work: evolution proceeds by means of dissociation (CE, 100/O, 579–80). This process is nothing other than the acts by which the multiplicity of the *élan vital* is actualized. Evolution proceeds through the differentiating movement of duration, which draws on the *élan vital* to create distinct tendencies.

While Bergson does not ascribe a common purpose to life, the *élan vital* is understood monistically. It is the very force from which life arises (CE, 51/O, 538). At this virtual source, all of the tendencies of life abided together because their features did not yet need to be differentiated. Even when Bergson speaks of the *élan vital* as a source, it must be understood as a multiplicity. In this sense, speaking of it as "one" or a "unity" is misleading. The only "thing" shared by all of the forces of the *élan vital* is the tendency to differentiate. In Bergson's vision of the Whole as an incalculable multiplicity of different degrees of tension, discussed earlier, the *élan vital* is virtually implied as the force of all of the different rhythms of duration.

Tendencies are not defined by the possession of particular attributes. On the contrary, they are characterized by the aspects that have the most emphasis. Animals, for instance, tend to accentuate movement while plants incline toward immobility. Most aspects of the Whole continue to abide in a specific tendency in a virtual state. "There is no manifestation of life which does not contain in a rudimentary state—either latent or virtual—the essential characters of most other manifestations" (translation modified; CE, 106/O, 585). In this sense, something of the virtual Whole abides in all of the dissociated tendencies that make up life (CE, 54/O, 540).

The first great bifurcation in Bergson's account of evolution is the division of the *élan vital* into life and matter. For Bergson, the reason for this dissociation is found in the divergent characters of these two tendencies. Life contains an unstable and explosive balance of forces to which inert matter is tremendously resistant (CE, 98/O, 578). Their dissociation enabled these antagonistic aspects of the *élan vital* to express themselves. It is should be remembered: the *élan vital* is virtual. It functions as the "reservoir" from which life engenders new tendencies, which in turn give rise to actualities. The emergence of matter and life, then, must be understood as an act of creation. When Bergson describes matter in negative terms, for instance, as the inversion or interruption of duration, he is speaking of it as a tendency distinguished from the inventive duration of life (CE, 186–271/O, 653–725; Deleuze B, 100–3). Bergsonian matter is construed as a positive fact. Yet it is precisely the antagonism between the explosive force of life and the rhythm of near necessity found in the force of matter that led to their bifurcation. Matter was an obstacle to life's creative dynamism.

The dissociation between life and matter is the first of many bifurcations in the movement of evolution. Although Bergson doesn't emphasize it, the first divergence within the tendency of life engenders what he calls "sexual generation." In a section of twelve pages devoted to the bifurcation between plant and animal, he makes a fleeting remark:

> Sexual generation is perhaps only a luxury for the plant, but to the animal it was a necessity, and the plant must have been driven to it by the same *élan* which impelled the animal thereto, a primitive, original *élan* anterior to the separation of the two kingdoms. (translation modified; CE 119/O, 596)

What I want to underline here is less the thesis that sexual reproduction is perhaps a luxury for plants than Bergson's admission that this bifurcation arises from a "primitive, original *élan*." He readily admits that not all of the directions of life hold the same interest for him. Bergson is particularly concerned with the path that leads to "Man" (*l'homme*) (CE, 105/O, 584). Bergson's treatise on evolution thus attends carefully to the dissociation between plant and animal and to the bifurcation between instinct and intellect. Yet his allusions to the emergence of sexual reproduction are few. Surely sexual generation occupies an important place in the path that leads to the human species?[5]

Bergson's marginalization of sexual generation is interesting in relation to the sexed hierarchy I suggest is at work in the images and metaphors he draws on to articulate his thought. In my view, emergence of the sexed hierarchy precedes the primitive *élan* that Bergson credits as the force that impels the emergence of sexual generation. I think it motivates the very desire to split the "antagonistic" forces of life and matter. While Bergson largely avoids an analysis of sexual generation, he repeatedly invokes images of ejaculation, explosion, and erection to account for the evolution of the life-and-matter relation.

Chapter Five analyzed Bergson's use in *Time and Free Will* of a paternal metaphor to describe the genesis of the free act. In *The Creative Evolution* he draws on the image of paternal creativity to elaborate another kind of free act, the organizing act. While the free act characterizes human consciousness, the organizing act is fundamentally transhuman; its source is the *élan vital*. This act is particularly important because it creates complex structures such as the human eye. Bergson writes:

> The organizing act . . . has something explosive about it: it needs at the beginning the smallest possible place, a minimum of matter, as if the organizing forces only entered space reluctantly. The spermatozoon, which sets in motion the evolutionary process of the embryonic life, is one of the smallest cells of the organism; and it is only a small part of the spermatozoon that really takes part in the operation. (CE, 92/O, 574)

This procreative image confers all of the creative force on the purely temporal act, which enters the space of matter "only reluctantly." In addition to emphasizing the immateriality of the organizing act, Bergson's image downplays the materiality of sperm. It is as though the truly creative aspect of sperm is not reducible to its material status.[6] This is, arguably, the most explicit use of a hierarchically sexed image in Bergson's account of evolution, yet there are many more instances in which he theorizes the relationship between life and matter in sexist terms, at least implicitly.

In a particularly puzzling formulation, Bergson suggests that life is an immaterial force making itself, while matter is unmaking itself. Matter's tendency toward spatiality, or what Bergson calls extension, can be understood as a temporal tension that is interrupted. He proposes that matter should be imagined as a falling weight (CE, 245/O, 703). Conversely life is a movement of ascent. These opposed movements must be understood together, especially given that, as Bergson admits, the creative activity of life evolves with matter on the surface of Earth. "If it were pure consciousness, *a fortiori* if it were supraconsciousness, it would be pure creative activity" (CE, 245/O, 703). This formulation suggests that life could exist independently of matter. Indeed, in the Huxley Lecture he makes precisely this claim (ME, 35/O, 835).[7]

The evolution of life on Earth has always been attached to matter. Life is "*riveted* to an organism that *subjects* [*la soumet*] it to the general laws of inert matter. But everything happens as if it were doing its upmost to set itself free" (CE, 245/O, 703). Bergson contends that life retards the descent of matter by acting on matter with its explosive energy. He turns to the cholorophyllous function of plants. Plants accumulate energy, as in a reservoir, that can be discharged suddenly through the nervous systems of the animals that eat them. Bergson hypothesizes that, prior to the dissociation between plant and animal, life was accumulating "explosives" to be released through movements. "It is like an effort to raise the weight which falls" (ME, 246/O, 704).

Matter is a weight that the explosive force of life attempts to mold and transform with tremendous effort. This scenario is reminiscent of a violently dichotomous figuration of heterosexual intercourse, in which a man rapes a woman whose inertia approaches "absolute passivity" (CE, 200/O, 665). Woman is figured here as an "inert" weight acted on by a frenzied man.

The phallocentrism of Bergson's life-matter relation is evident also in a number of images that he proposes for understanding the relation between them. He invokes his readers to think of a vessel full of steam at high pressure. The vessel has a few cracks and steam escapes its enclosure, in a jet:

> The steam shot [*lance*] into the air is nearly all condensed into little drops which fall back [*retombent*], and this condensation and this fall [*chute*] represent simply the loss of something, an interruption, a deficit. But a small part of the jet stream subsists, uncondensed, for some seconds; it is making an effort to raise the drops which are falling (*tombent*); it succeeds at most in retarding [*ralentir*] their fall [*la chute*]. So, from an immense reservoir of life, jets must be shooting out [*s'élancer*] unceasingly, of which each falling back [*retombent*] is a world. [Translation modified] (CE, 247/O, 705)

Bergson warns against taking this comparison too far. The cracks, the jets of steam, the forming of the drops are subject to the laws of inert matter, and the creation of a world is a free act. He proposes instead the image of the action of an arm raising itself. For Bergson, the effort to lift the arm gives a better sense of life's freedom, while the tendency of the arm to fall back down reveals the direction of matter unmaking this effort. "In this image of a *creative action which unmakes itself* we . . . have a more exact representation of [animate] matter" (CE, 247–8/O, 705). This image, like that of jet stream shooting forth from a vessel, is reminiscent of a penis becoming erect in arousal and falling back into detumescence. And Bergson proposes yet another metaphor with strongly phallic connotations. "Consciousness or supraconsciousness is the name for the rocket whose extinguished fragments (*les debris*) fall back as matter; consciousness . . . is . . . that which subsists of the rocket itself, passing through the fragments and lighting them up into organisms" (CE, 261/O, 716).

"Inert" matter is the debris of the *élan vital*'s immense effort to create. Some of this debris gets animated by the passage of consciousness through "it" and thus engenders organisms. However, it is the tendency of life itself that is credited as the true creator of the living being.

These passages demonstrate the valorization of a hypermasculine theory of life and corresponding devaluation of matter as feminine. This is not a binary hierarchy, because Bergson's concepts of life and matter are never actualized as pure activity and pure space. He emphasizes that there is always a trace of the characteristics of most other tendencies within any of the actualized tendencies of life (CE, 106/O, 585). For this reason, matter's inclination toward pure repetition is never fully achieved. There are some oscillations in matter's rhythm that are analogous to the dynamic transformations articulated in the duration of life. At the same time, life is not manifested as pure creative energy. Life is riveted to matter and can actualize free acts only through its inverse tendency. Moreover, Bergson admits that, if materiality was pure repetition, life could never have installed itself within matter's palpitations. In an important passage from the Huxley Lecture, he writes:

> Life would be impossible were the determination of matter so absolute as to admit of no relaxation. Suppose, however, that at particular moments and at particular points matter shows a certain elasticity, then and there will be the opportunity for consciousness to install itself. It will have to humble itself at first; yet, once installed, it will dilate, it will spread from its point of entry and not rest till it has conquered [*obtenir*] the whole, for time is at its disposal, and the slightest quantity of indetermination, by continually adding to itself, will make up as much freedom as you like.[8] (ME, 18/O, 824–25)

At particular moments, matter "offers a certain elasticity" that allows life to transform it. Life could never have succeeded in creating organisms without the emergence of these fluctuations at certain points within matter's rhythm. From this passage there emerge a number of important questions that Bergson does not address. Why does matter generate fluctuations in its rhythm? Is elasticity merely a fortuitous accident, or are the oscillations in matter provoked when consciousness seeks to install an action on it? Does this imply that matter anticipates the imminence of a new act, which exceeds the plane of actuality that Bergson frequently insists matter is confined to? We could say what Bergson does not say: when the force of life stimulates matter, it does not merely repeat its past. Matter actualizes alterations in its tension that constitute new configurations in the becoming of the world. But this is still to accept the terms of Bergson's dualism. Perhaps we would do better to reconsider the life–matter relation beyond dualism?

Let us return to what Bergson *says* in this quotation. Far from modifying the violent hierarchy of life over matter by allowing matter, however infinitesimally, to participate in engendering new actualities in the world, Bergson declares that material elasticity allows life to install itself. Once life (*la conscience*) has entered matter, "it will not rest until it has conquered the whole" (ME, 18/O, 824). In sexed terms, matter's elasticity makes her amenable to the power of the masculine tendency to create. She offers herself to life and allows him "to conquer" (*obtenir*) her.

Given the sexual violence of Bergson's figuration of the life–matter relation, it is no surprise to find him asserting that the subjugation of matter is most successful in "Man" (*l'homme*). In the same essay, Bergson praises "man alone" for his ability to force matter into the status of a "mere instrument" (*à l'état d'instrument*). He has this ability because to every habit he has contracted he can oppose a contrary habit, and this gives him more freedom than any other animate creature has to act on matter.[9] In other organisms, freedom remains riveted to the "chains" of matter. At most they are able to "stretch these chains." But, in Man, "a sudden bound (*un saut brusque*) is made." Freedom is unleashed. "Freedom, coming to itself whilst necessity is at grips with itself, brings back matter to the condition of being a mere instrument. It is as though it has divided in order to rule" (ME, 26/O, 830).

For Bergson, Man is distinguished from animals by a difference in nature and presented as the "end" of evolution. He warns his readers that Man is the "end" in a special sense. Bergson does not mean to imply that Man's success realizes a ready-made plan. The divergent actualizations of the *élan vital* were contingent and radically unpredictable. Man is only one species among a number of them. Nonetheless, Man is the great success of evolution because he alone allowed life to finally triumph over the "obstacle" of matter (CE, 263–66/O, 718–21). Despite his argument to the contrary, Bergson's celebration of Man as the "end" of evolution tends to undercut the innovation for which his philosophy is justly famous: the claim that duration articulates an incalculable flow of novelty (CE, 266/O, 720–21).

Keith Ansell-Pearson has voiced grave reservations about these humanist assertions in Bergson's corpus. According to Ansell-Pearson, Bergson's evolutionary philosophy elevates the "form" of Man in a gesture of "residual perfectionism" (Ansell-Pearson 1999, 158–59). I support Ansell-Pearson's call to move beyond the "residual perfectionism" and "anthropocentrism" at work in this aspect of Bergson's oeuvre (Ansell-Pearson 1999, 159). But it is not just a case of exceeding the problematic elevation of "Man" in Bergsonism. The privilege conferred on life as a movement of ascent and creation and the simultaneous degradation of matter as an obstacle to the progress of life must be called into question. This violent hierarchy articulates a kind of phallic anthropomorphism, where matter is the stuff or dead weight that paternal life must impregnate or overcome in order to incarnate animate beings and introduce free acts into the world. At his most extreme, Bergson valorizes a spiritual position that is nothing short of somataphobic. He speculates that human consciousness may have "an intenser life" no longer riveted to the body (ME, 35/O, 835).

BECOMING CONCRETE EXTENSITY

Perhaps difference is not sexed. But given the way that Bergson's philosophy of vital difference insistently asserts "itself" as phallocentrism, taking up his thinking requires a revaluation of the feminine as something other than a passive resource for the masculine. It also entails a revaluation of the masculine as something other than the explosive, creative action of evolutionary differentiation. Before attempting to think sexual difference with Bergson, I want to make some suggestions on how to reelaborate the life–matter relationship. This task is obviously related to the question of sexual difference, though the implications of this reelaboration are not reducible to the question of sexual difference. I hope it has value for thinkers interested in affirming the duration and inventive capacities of matter.

De Landa's Deleuzian inspired thought provides significant insight into the revaluation of Bergsonian materiality. Drawing on Deleuze and complexity theory, de Landa argues that matter is able to exceed the tendency toward entropy in far from equilibrium conditions. In these instances, "inert" matter is capable of organizing itself and acting in ways that exceed a rhythm of repetition "to express itself in complex and creative ways" (de Landa 1992, 133).

To affirm the creative capacity of matter is to challenge Bergson's figuration of the virtual and the actual. In Bergson, the virtual at its limit is a purely intensive, spiritual concept, while the actual at its limit is pure extensity and indistinguishable from homogeneous space. Contra Bergson, de Landa suggests that the virtual arises from the duration of matter. This does not mean that the virtual is actualized; it means that the virtual has a material foundation or, better, that it is generated from the rhythms of material becoming.[10] Living reality is always a mixture of the virtual and actual or of duration and materiality.

Instead of speaking of the life–matter relation we should, perhaps, speak of the becoming of concrete extensity. The phrase "becoming of concrete extensity" must not be read in opposition to "life" or "supraconsciousness." Material becoming is coincident with life, "the machinic phylum is materiality, natural or artificial, and both simultaneously; it is matter in movement, in flux, in variation, matter as conveyor of singularities and traits of expression" (Deleuze and Guattari 1987, 409).

The affirmation of the palpitations of materiality as the expressive substance of life in all of its divergent articulations amounts to a redistribution of the way in which the concepts of life and matter operate in Bergsonism. Where Bergson usually splits these concepts,

I am suggesting they must be kept together. This is not strictly unfaithful to his thought. In *Matter and Memory*, he describes the Whole as "concrete extensity" pervaded by "*modifications, perturbations* changes of *tension* or of *energy* and nothing else" (MM, 201). In this monistic formulation, life and matter are thought together as enduring tensions, as difference, actualizing the new.

THE TENDENCIES OF SEXUAL DIFFERENCE

Grosz has argued that feminist theory should take up the concept of force as a way of moving beyond the strictures of the subject and beyond the constraints of human being. Force is inhuman. It is the very condition of emergence of the human, sexual identities, social practices and institutions (TT, 186–87). Thinking in these terms is to not to deny sexual difference but to resituate it. She writes:

> This profusion of energies and forces functioning within and as subjects is not the denial of sexual difference but its increasing elaboration, for sexual difference, the systematically differentiated morphologies of (most) living bodies, operate not only at the level of the body-as-a-whole, but also within the body's microscopic functions and processes. (TT, 195)

Each sex is a specific multiplicity of forces operating within subjects and in radical excess of them. The sexes operate microscopically and macroscopically. They function at the organic level and, beyond the organic forms of living bodies, as pre-individuated forces in the becoming of life and matter. In this formulation, the interval of sexual difference is a differentiating movement that articulates the tendencies of the masculine and the tendencies of the feminine as specific rhythms of differentiation. The interval of sexual difference is neither specifically human nor tied to the definition of individuals but is rather implied in the proliferation and mutation of species that reproduce through sexual generation.

The forces of sexuate becoming can be contrasted to the microfeminine particle warfare described by Luciana Parisi in *Abstract Sex*. Like Grosz's concept of inhuman force, Parisi's microfeminine particle warfare articulates a passage of becoming without a subject. For Parisi, what defines microfeminine particle warfare as feminine is the fluidity of the process of becoming.

> Femininity no longer remains specific to one mode of sex. It is not localized in one body or another, in one composition or another. It is not an identity, an individual unity. Feminine desire can only be defined by a pack of relations where microfeminine particle-forces spread at every kinetic encounter. These relations produce a micropolitics of becoming where particle-forces combine or disintegrate, activate or react against new encounters. (Parisi 2004, 39)

For Parisi, the feminine is a process combining the most indifferent elements that is distinguished from a logic that fixates on the substance of things. In her terms, the unpredictable and expressive behavior of matter in far from equilibrium conditions, as described by de Landa, is an instance of femininity. I don't want to deny the importance of a project explicitly opposed to phallocentrism and what Gilles Deleuze calls macropolitics. But the antiessentialist conception of feminine differentiation elaborated by Parisi must be distinguished from the thinking of *sexual* difference. For me and for Grosz—at least as I read her—a feminine force of becoming *is* defined by organic components of the female sex. Here the female sex refers not to a subject but to sex cells, hormonal rhythms, and the expression of sexuate body parts. So while the feminine is not dependent on the identity of a female subject, female becoming does designate substantial material organizations.

Grosz emphasizes that the becoming of a force always involves struggle and combat against other forces. In one sense this is a combative struggle against other forces; it is also the process by which forces merge, mutate, and join with other forces (TT, 188). The interactions between the forces in a becoming can be conceived in terms of an ethics of relations. Here ethics no longer designates a relation between "two subjects," it is an ethics of relations within and between forces beyond the order of number. We need an ethics of the multiplicity of forces in the becoming of the feminine, an ethics of the multiplicity of forces in the becoming of the masculine, and an ethics of their mixing together in intersexed becoming.

In a subjective context Irigaray has argued persuasively that the female sex was never especially passive (ESD/E). More broadly her work unravels a naïve opposition between pure activity and pure passivity. This has important implications for reconceiving sexual difference in relation to Bergson's philosophy. Instead of thinking the differentiation of the tendencies of sexual difference in terms of a tendency to activity and a tendency to passivity (as Bergson does in his anthropomorphization of life and matter), I contend that each sex is active-passive. The generative rhythms of the sexes are active-passive in palpitations, repetitions, and oscillations that are irreducible to one another. As tendencies, the multiplicity of forces in each sex implies the virtuality of the other sex within "itself."

To suggest that sexual difference can be conceived as the becoming of specific tendencies is not to surpass the task of articulating sexed intersubjectivity through the interval. It offers another way of conceptualizing sexual difference that reveals, perhaps, an anthropocentric bias in Irigaray's sexed ethics. But this is not entirely fair to Irigaray, because, as I have argued throughout this book, her formulation of the interval is irreducibly open. The intersubjective figuration of sexual difference elaborated by Irigaray and the conceptualization of sexed becoming sketched through a reading of Grosz should not be placed in competition. It is important for feminists to invent multiple passages for thinking sexual difference. While these approaches diverge on the status of the centrality of human being to the thinking of sexual difference, they also converge precisely in the effort to conceive difference as a place of open potentiality.

Conclusion: Interval as Relation, Interval as Becoming

> It is obvious that any form is precarious, since it depends on relations between forces and their mutations.
>
> DELEUZE 1988, 129

FOR IRIGARAY, the interval is difference, the threshold from which space and time and matter and form are engendered (IR, 166–7/E, 15). The concepts of space and time and matter and form are abstract and by no means restricted in the Western tradition to theorizing sexual difference. I have argued that Irigaray acknowledges the possibility of conceiving difference prior to and in excess of sexual difference, if she is read carefully. She suggests that sexual difference is "perhaps the most unthinkable of differences, difference itself" (WL, 106). To deploy the open potentiality of the "perhaps" is to admit the necessary possibility of conceiving difference otherwise, beyond the question of sexual difference. In other words, the focus on *sexual* difference in Irigaray is a focus of emphasis rather than a denial of the primacy of other modalities of difference.[1]

Given that the interval is a necessarily open threshold, the effacement of the interval in traditional metaphysics cannot only be a failure to articulate nonhierarchical sexual difference. In principle, the obfuscation of the interval generates an incalculable "number" of structural hierarchies.

Irigaray's approach to thinking the interval of sexual difference tends to address sexual difference, especially in her later work, in terms of human being. This is not to say that human being precedes the interval, for the interval in Irigaray is precisely the differentiating movement that articulates humanity as sexed, as woman and man. What is the value of this specific approach to difference?

This question is especially pertinent in relation to Bergson and Aristotle. Both of these philosophers' projects elaborate theories of space and time and matter and form that are intended to account for reality in the broadest sense. Bergson in particular establishes a concept of the interval beyond the demands of human practical experience, demands that, he argues, have secretly determined metaphysical speculation. He posits his figuration of the interval as the opening to the intuition of life and duration (MM, 184–85/O, 320). From this perspective, developing an approach to the interval that is no longer primarily concerned with sexuate human being would be more faithful to Bergson's legacy and would have wider implications than an avowedly anthropocentric pursuit of the question of sexual difference between woman and man.

The problem for Irigaray is that the sexuation of knowledge cannot be easily put aside in order to pursue a form of knowledge beyond the decisive turn of human experience. Irigaray believes Western philosophy has engendered a sexuate relation. More precisely, metaphysics has been posited on the basis of covering over a sexuate relation: knowledge is presented as phallomorphism through the disavowal of its relation to the maternal-feminine, philosophy's secret condition. The differentiating relation enabling metaphysics is also buried. This work confirms the stakes of her critical description, at least in the case of Aristotle and Bergson. Both of these philosophers' oeuvres tend to elide the possibility of thinking the interval, albeit in markedly different ways, and valorize hierarchically sexed theories of space and time and matter and form.

To say that Aristotle and Bergson tend to articulate phallomorphisms or phallic anthropomorphisms is not to condemn their projects. There are in their thinking countertendencies that can be read as undermining phallomorphism and as contributing to a philosophy of difference and sexual difference. What are these countertendencies?

In a crucial moment of *Physics* 4, Aristotle affirms *topos*—a relation between two bodies that differ in being—as the opening of his system (210a24). Taken out of context, this would be a surprising assertion, because Aristotle is infamous for (claiming) to subordinate difference to the identity of the categories (9998b24–27). I have argued that his reduction of difference to identity is predicated on a form of sexual violence whereby all of the privileged concepts of his ontology—form, identity, substance, and *physis*—are isomorphically congruent with a phallic conception of man, while the devalorized concepts in his discourse, which cannot even be said to be—matter and privation—are marked as feminine and traces with remainders of the maternal-feminine (726a34–b1, 728a26–30, 737a27–29, 192a14–23, 193b12, 193b7–8). And yet he contradicts the hierarchical structure of his system by affirming the foundational status of difference at a number of loci in his discourse.

In *Metaphysics* 3, Aristotle admits that difference has being prior to the identity of any of the categories (998b22–23). In *Physics* 4, he affirms that the contiguous status of a thing in place—a sensible relation between two bodies that differ in being—precedes the being of the form in the definition, the very constituents of the identity of his highest concept, substance (210s15–24). This assertion is significant because Aristotle specifies that difference is a *spatial relation* between bodies. This figuration can be understood as an affirmation of the embodied and differential nature of thinking.

At this moment in his corpus, Aristotle posits the knowledge of the lived sensible relation between two different bodies as the opening of thinking. My affirmation of the embodied, spatial, and relational nature of the interval is not intended to reduce the interval to a calculable gap in homogeneous space or to the inflexible form of a definition. Aristotle explicitly distinguishes place—the relationship between a body and the *topos* circumscribing that body—from the homogeneous space of geometrical calculation (193b24–194a1).

I am not suggesting that my deconstructive reading of Aristotle articulates a differential relation as such. After all, he asserts that the limit between place and body defines *topos*, which he insists is immobile (212a20–21). The nature of the sensible relation *as a relation* is undermined by the pronounced presentism of this figuration. From this perspective, Bergson might object that Aristotle remains more committed to Euclidean space than he acknowledges. For the conception of body and place together as self present to one another obliterates heterogeneity and allows for the possibility of a calculation that specifies this limit in a grid of geometrical space.

The consequences of this are disastrous for the temporal nature of the interval. Irigaray's rereading of Aristotle implies a way to overcome the presentism of his argument. She turns to Aristotle's account of *topos* in order to conceive the lived spatiality of sexed subjects (ESD, 34–55/E, 41–59). Irigaray rereads Aristotle's formulation to suggest that place—or woman—is not an immobile limit surrounding the man-embryo but an open envelope, a place in multiple senses. She also argues that man must be conceived as an envelope that remains open to functioning as place in several senses. These two envelopes, like Aristotle's figuration of a thing and the *topos* surrounding the thing, are conceived as different in being. In contrast to Aristotle's formulation, she does not construe woman and man as self present to one another. They are engendered in relation to each other through the interval, which is not an immobile limit but an enduring threshold that is nothing other than the condition of woman and man's potential to be.

Irigaray's radicalization of Aristotle does not explicitly posit a theory of time. Bergson's painstaking elaboration of duration offers important insight into understanding the temporal dynamics of the interval of sexual difference. His work demonstrates that Aristotle's figuration of *topos* as a present relation between bodies brings back homogeneous space to cover over the possibility of thinking the places of bodies as they exist in nature beyond the imposition of mathematical calculation. For Bergson the interval is never given; the interval is a threshold to the past and to the open potentiality of coming to be.

Bergson's interval is a flow of purely qualitative change distinguished from the repetitive rhythms of matter by a difference in nature. I have contested this figuration of difference in Bergson and argued with de Landa, Deleuze, and Guattari that the duration of the interval must be thought with materiality.

My disagreement with Bergsonian dualism is fundamentally informed by Irigaray's feminist radicalization of Aristotelian hylomorphism. Matter and form are brought together by the interval, the place of desire. Matter is shaped by form, but matter is by no means subordinate in this formation. What impels form is not a lack in matter but the generative interval *between* form and matter. And the interval always remains in play, ceaselessly inducing new formations and reformations. Matter and form entwine with each other in attractions, tensions, and acts that are never accomplished (IR, 167–68; ESD, 8, 48; 49/E, 15–16, 53, 54). This Irigarayan postulation far exceeds the sexuation of human mortals. It also suggests her specific focus on difference, as *sexual* difference has value in the impossible task of conceiving difference, beyond specifically feminist concerns. While Irigaray does not spell it out, the very openness of her formulation of the interval demonstrates in principle that it must function potentially as a threshold of prehuman and posthuman differentiation.

At his best Bergson undermines his own habit of opposing matter and duration. In *Matter and Memory* he posits a thinking of difference and matter that has some resonance with Irigaray's transvaluation of Aristotle. He affirms "concrete extensity" pervaded by "*modifications, perturbations,* changes of *tension* or of *energy* and nothing else" (MM, 201). In this monistic formulation the duration of life and matter are thought together as enduring tensions, as difference, ceaselessly actualizing the new.

The rhythms of concrete extensity can be understood as the rhythms from which the interval of sexual difference is conceived as the interval of becoming. Drawing on Grosz, this book has argued that the interval of sexual difference is the engendering force not only of sexed human subjects but of nonhuman animals, social practices, and institutions. Beyond these organic forms, the interval as becoming is also understood as the threshold of emergence of microscopic functions and processes within and in excess of organic bodies. The interval of sexual difference in this sense is a multiplicity of sexed forces articulating the tendencies of the masculine and the tendencies of the feminine as specific rhythms of differentiation.

At first glance, the figuration of the interval as a threshold of becoming might be read to undermine Irigaray's inclination to construe difference as the sexed relation between woman and man. But an attentive reading of Irigaray reveals no contradiction between thinking difference as relation and thinking difference as becoming. The figuration of the relationship between subjects (an intersubjective approach) is an elaboration of becoming. For example, the threshold between a woman and a man is a relation in which each sex is in becoming in relation to the self and in becoming in relation to the other sex. The interval, the force that engenders their being, is an excess that persists beyond the actualization of any specific relation as the possibility of other becomings. To put this in Bergsonian terms, the intersubjective relation generated by the interval is always traced with the virtual mutations of other potential actualizations.

The interval of becoming is also a threshold of relations. The becoming of the feminine, for instance, consists of a multiplicity of forces converging, diverging, and mutating. The difference in tension between these forces acting and reacting together can be conceived in terms of relations. Here "relation" no longer designates a relationship between "two" subjects but an economy of relations within and between forces, outside the order of number.

The forms posited of Irigaray's intersubjective becoming are different, of course, from the forms emphasized in the anti-subjective and avowedly posthuman trajectory of sexual difference. But these approaches differ by virtue of the figures they articulate and the specific problems they address rather than because they emerge from different conceptions of the interval. The accomplishment of the interval always remains in reserve.

NOTES

INTRODUCTION

1. *The Oxford English Dictionary*, 2nd ed., s.v. "interval" 1, 2, 3, 6. *Nouveau petit Robert dictionnaire de la langue française*, s.v. "intervalle" 1, 3.

2. The interval of sexual difference has been addressed directly by a number of Irigaray's readers but not in booklength studies. Scholars I know of who have addressed the interval explicitly include, Tina Chanter (EE, 152; 158), Cheah (FSD, 27–8; 33; 36–37), Rosalyn Diprose (1994, 37), David Farrell-Krell (1997, 161–71), Helen Fielding (2003, 13), Elizabeth Grosz (1994, 208–9; 2001, 157–8), Dorothea Olkowski (RR, 80–3; BI), Gail Schwab (1994, 362–372), and Ewa Plonowska Ziarek (2001, 152–3, 159–72).

3. Dianne Perpich has compared Irigaray and Adriana Caverero on the basis of what Perpich frames as a grounding concern in both of their oeuvres with the question of "who speaks?" See Perpich, 2003. Claire Colebrook characterizes Irigaray as a thinker of subjectivity in "Is Sexual Difference a Problem?" (1999b), and Grosz cites Colebrook's characterization of Irigaray as a thinker of subjectivity in "Inhuman Forces" (*TT*). The argument of my article "Interval, Sexual Difference" also unduly restricts Irigarayan sexual difference to a thinking of sexed subjectivity (Hill, 2008).

4. Irigaray's critical description of metaphysics as phallocentric is well known. In Chapter One, I develop a detailed account of her critique of Western philosophy by concentrating on her reading of Aristotle. General accounts of the broad sweep of Irigaray's argument are well handled by Margaret Whitford (1991, 30–52), Cathryn Vasseleu (1998, 8–11), and Grosz (1989, 104–10).

5. I am sympathetic to the position of Ellen Mortensen on the way in which "difference" is often construed in feminist theory. She writes: "During the last two decades feminist theory has been caught up in endless theoretical elaboration on possible identifications of 'difference,' posited either as objects of epistemology or as dominant characteristics of the identity of groups or individuals. This has resulted in a paradoxical state of affairs: the more insistent they have been in the affirmation of 'difference,' the more monotonous, repetitious and predictable the discussions have become. In many of these feminist studies 'difference' constitutes more of a theoretical *doxa* than a thoughtful consideration of radical alterity" (2002, 1).

6. Olkowski's reading of Bergson and Irigaray effectively points out the fundamental importance of the interval to their respective projects, but Olkowski does not address the divergences between Irigaray and Bergson. I argue at length in Chapter Six that these divergences are significant (RR, 80–3; BI). Grosz does not offer a detailed account of the relationship between Bergsonian qualitative difference (what I call the interval) and the Irigarayan interval of sexual difference. Like Olkowski, though, Grosz affirms a strong affinity between Bergson and Irigaray. In the introduction to *The Nick of Time*, Grosz suggests that Irigaray "develops, perhaps more than any other writer since Bergson, a practical metaphysics that rigorously develops Bergsonian intuition as its primary method" (14). I disagree. The relationship between Irigaray's approach to the question of sexual difference and Bergsonian intuition is more fraught than Grosz suggests. This difficult relationship is addressed in Chapters Five and Six and the Conclusion.

1. THE OBLIVION OF THE INTERVAL

1. Unless otherwise indicated, all references to Aristotle are drawn from *The Complete Works of Aristotle*, ed. Jonathan Barnes, rev. trans., 2 volumes (Princeton: Princeton University Press, 1984).

2. Tina Chanter and Penelope Deutscher have argued that Irigaray's relation to Aristotle's philosophy is complex. That is to say, while Irigaray is tremendously critical of Aristotle, her texts are also indebted to certain concepts in his work, especially place (*lieu, topos*) (Chanter EE, 151–59; Deutscher ID, 114).

3. Jay citing Dewey (1938, 192). See Jay 1981, 44.

4. See Derrida's well-known remarks in the interviews "Choreographies" (1985, 183–85) and "Women in the Beehive" (1989, 198). In these texts, Derrida distinguishes between sexual opposition (man/woman) and sexual difference. According to his formulation, sexual difference goes beyond dualism to affirm an incalculable number of sexes.

5. Derrida's construal of sexual opposition as "two" is very close to Irigaray's understanding of binary oppositions. He would agree that the devalued term in a dualism is the negation of the valorized term. Derrida diverges from Irigaray insofar as he is suspicious of advocating sexual difference as "two." He fears that this figuration may fall back into a hierarchical dichotomy. Yet there is perhaps a moment of equivocation on this point; when pressed by Christie McDonald, Derrida suggests a radical figuration of sexual difference as "doubly dissymmetrical." For Derrida, "[sexual difference] remains no doubt irreducibly dissymmetrical . . . a certain dissymmetry is no doubt the law of both sexual difference and the relationship to the other in general" (1985, 184–5).

6. Heidegger's revolutionary work on the ontico-ontological difference is a touchstone and inspiration for three of the French philosophers named here: Derrida, Deleuze, and Irigaray. The exception, of course, is Bergson whose articulation of qualitative difference precedes Heidegger's groundbreaking *Being and Time*

by about thirty years. These five thinkers are by no means the only philosophers to decry the subordination of difference to identity. But their work is outstanding for its influence in contemporary continental philosophy and feminist theory. See Heidegger 1969; Derrida MP, 3–27; and Deleuze 1994, 30–35.

7. I could have written "the phallus" here, but I wanted to underscore the relation of phallocentrism to the male sex organ. See Irigaray's famous essay, the title piece of *This Sex Which Is Not One*, where she writes: "The more or less exclusive—and highly anxious—attention paid to erection in Western sexuality proves to what extent the imaginary that governs it is foreign to the feminine. For the most part, this sexuality offers nothing but imperatives dictated by male rivalry: the 'strongest' being the one who has the best 'hard-on', the longest, the biggest, the stiffest penis, or even the one who 'pees the farthest' (as in little boys' contests)" (TS, 24–25). These comments arise in a debate with Freud and Lacan but they are, also more broadly, intended as a critique of the unavowed masculinism of metaphysics. Also, Irigaray says the penis is the empirical representative of ideal functioning (TS, 110).

8. My discussion in this section is drawn primarily from the *Metaphysics*. A number of the most respected Aristotle scholars have concluded that the fourteen books making up this treatise were composed over a long period. These scholars argue that within each book sections were added and changed as Aristotle revised and developed his thinking. From this perspective, contradictions between different books in the *Metaphysics* can be understood as evidence of the evolution of Aristotle's philosophy. I will not seek to smooth over the manifest contradictions in his discourse on the basis that they were probably composed at different times. For me, the incompatibility between, for example, the definition of difference found in the fifth book (an early text) and the discussion of complete difference in book 10 (a late text) is interesting, because it reveals uncertainty and hesitation in his engagement with a tremendously complex problem. In other words, these stammerings in Aristotle are fruitful for thinking difference. See Hugh Tredennick's comments in the introduction to his translation of the *Metaphysics* 1–9 in Aristotle 1933, xxxi–xxxiii. Also see Ross 1964, 17; G. E. R. Lloyd 1968, 15; and Herbert Granger 1984, 1–2.

9. The last two examples provided here are drawn from Kenneth Itzkowitz 1982, 341. Of course, there is still a sense in which the sacrifice of Iphigenia and the clock can be related: both have being.

10. Olkowski's claim that "Aristotle is completely unwilling to count as differences those differences that are merely other and do not differ in a particular respect" deserves qualification here. In the context of *Metaphysics* 10 she is right, but in the earlier treatise *Metaphysics* 5 otherness is allowed a share of difference (Olkowski RR, 18).

11. Differences within species are permitted provided they do not alter the definition of the species-form, which in Aristotle's terms must be a unity. See the following paragraph in the main text.

12. It is interesting to note that Aristotle makes no mention of differences predicated on the basis of analogical identity that he describes in *Metaphysics* 5. Nonetheless, according to Franz Brentano in his influential book *The Several Senses of Being in Aristotle*, analogy is crucial to Aristotle because it enables him to assert that being is a unity—to assert this while not describing it as a kind of higher genus in which all the categories (generic kinds) would be contained (Brentano 1975, 60–66). Also, see the next two endnotes.

13. In the *Topics* and the *Categories*, Aristotle lists ten genera. Being is said to be a substance (*ousia*), a quantity (*poson*), a quality (*poion*), a relation (*pros ti*), a where (*pou*), a when (*pote*), a posture (*keisthai*), a having (*echein*), a doing (*poien*), and a being affected (*paschein*) (1a–15b32; 103b21–22). There are a couple of points to note about this list. In these early texts, Aristotle does not use the words *topos* and *chronos* but refers to *pou* and *pote* respectively. It is in the *Physics* that *topos* and *chronos* become the names of these categories. Second, Brentano points out that "it has been widely accepted that Aristotle quietly abandoned two of the original ten categories, namely posture [*keisthai*] and having [*echein*], which were originally introduced only because of the old Pythagorean and Platonic preference for the number ten" (1975, 50).

14. I owe the last point to Olkowski (RR, 20). The entire passage in which Aristotle makes these paradoxical remarks is extraordinary. Aristotle admits that, if a genus were a predicate of difference, then the number of principles would be practically infinite, especially if we supposed the highest genus to be a principle. The highest genus, which Aristotle does not allow, would render being univocal, which, for Aristotle, it is not (998b14–999a23). See Brentano 1975, 60–66; Olkowski RR, 19–20; and Deleuze 1994, 33–4.

15. In addition to Irigaray's work on Aristotle's sexist dualism, see Genevieve Lloyd, 1984, 7–9; Butler 1993, 27–55; Charlotte Witt (1999) and Marguerite Deslauriers (1999). Aristotle's account of the form–matter relation is related to his account of reproduction, which has also attracted extensive feminist criticism. See Jay 1981, 46; Ward 1996; Bat-Ami Bar On 1994; Nancy Tuana 1989.

16. Fielding (2003) is a notable exception to this tendency. Apart from Fielding, there are a couple of readings of Irigaray's thinking on nature, but they are not developed in specific relation to Aristotle or *physis*. See Grosz and Cheah OBT, 8–10, and Stone 2003.

17. Clarendon translation (1983b).

18. The example of wood is particularly pertinent, as "wood" is an earlier meaning of *hylē*, as Judith Butler has emphasized (1993, 31). See also *A Greek–English Lexicon*, 8th ed., s.v. "hylē."

19. Clarendon translation (1983b).

20. Clarendon translation (1983b).

Aristotle regularly moves between two words for form: *morphē* and *eidos*. Ross explains that *morphē* is used for sensible shape. For example, it is *morphē* that a sculptor imposes on "his" [*sic*] material (*hylē*) to make a statue. *Eidos* implies form in the sense of intelligible structure and is synonymous with *logos* (formula or definition) and *to ti ēn einai* ("the what it is to be so-and-so"). *Morphē*, on Ross's reading, is clearly related to *eidos*, although *eidos* has privilege because it is the word with which Aristotle denotes the intelligible form (1964, 74). Heidegger argues that *morphē* must be understood in accordance with *eidos* and that *eidos* must be understood in relation to *logos* (1998, 210). For Heidegger, these concepts are not synonyms. There is, nonetheless, a primordial relation between *morphē*, *eidos*, and *logos*. Lear, like Heidegger, underlines the importance of *logos* to understanding form. While *logos* is sometimes translated as "definition," it can also be translated as "order," "ratio," "proportion," and "arrangement." When Aristotle says that form is the "logos of the essence [*ousia*]," he means that form instantiates an arrangement or an intelligible order that gives the essence of a thing, whether that thing is due to art or *physis* (194b27; Lear 1988, 28–29). I found Lear's discussion helpful here, though he does not distinguish between *eidos* and *morphē*. His argument would seem to suggest, though, that he is discussing *eidos*, which has the stronger connotation of intelligibility. Given that Aristotle uses *morphē* and *eidos* interchangeably in these difficult passages from the *Physics*, it seems Heidegger is right to relate *morphē* to *eidos*.

21. See Ross 1964, 182–86, and especially Lear 1988, 293–320.

22. He says that "matter is unknowable in itself."

23. Clarendon translation (1983b).

24. There is within Aristotle scholarship an interesting debate on this very passage. Brentano disputes the tendency of his contemporaries (which, by the way, is followed by the twentieth-century Aristotle specialists Ross and Charlton) to ascribe desire to matter. As Brentano puts it, these scholars argue that matter desires form in order to become similar to the deity (*theos*). For Brentano, "If it is thought that corporeal matter achieves actuality through a literal desire for the deity, then one must suppose that, above all, this matter thinks of the deity." On Brentano's argument this is impossible, because "prime matter is not supposed to have thoughts even of sensible things, let alone of an intelligible thing such as the deity." Instead, Brentano suggests that Aristotle uses "desire" metaphorically. For example, "instead of saying that the wheelwright put grease on the wheel to reduce friction, we say that the axle grease seeks to reduce friction" (Brentano 1978, 76–77). In this sense, Aristotle's doctrine can be interpreted to mean that it is the deity's will that impels matter to achieve the actuality of form.

Brentano's thesis is not without its own problems. Aristotle says explicitly that form cannot desire because it is not defective (192a20–21). Now the deity is the highest principle in Aristotle's thought. "He" is perfect and uncreated. In other words, if the deity lacks nothing, why then would the deity desire the improvement of something as degraded and corruptible as matter (Brentano 1978, 76–77)? Also see Ross in Aristotle 1936, 498; and Charlton in Aristotle 1970, 82–83.

25. These comments on the entrainment of concept and metaphor are indebted to Vasseleu 1998, 3–18.

26. As I argue below, however, there is also a sense in which the female is figured as privation in the *Generation of Animals*.

27. The sexist stakes of the loathing of matter Grosz deplores in *Volatile Bodies* (1994) are unmistakable here.

28. Aristotle's doctrine of causality is by no means restricted to reproduction. It is applied to all kinds of changes. In the case of an artificial production, wood is classed as the primary substrate, and the shape of a table is its form or efficient cause. The moving cause is the movement applied to wood by a carpenter to make a table. The final cause is the purpose of the table—for example, a raised flat surface that can be used to write or eat at (Lloyd AGS, 59–60). For a more detailed analysis of the four causes, see Lloyd AGS, 57–62, and Lear 1988, 28–42.

29. Irigaray is particularly attentive to the girl's status here; indeed the title of her essay is presented as an open question to Aristotle: "How to Conceive (of) a Girl?" (*Comment concevoir une fille?*). Strangely, the translators of *Speculum of the Other Woman* (1985b) dropped Irigaray's question mark from the English title, which is unfortunate because it is central to her argument. If a girl is engendered only through a sort of aberration or accident, then how can she exist?

The constraints of space do not permit me to go into a more detailed analysis of sexual reproduction in Aristotle. Briefly, the fundamental principle of generation is vital heat, which is contained within the intellect (*pneuma*) in the immaterial aspect of semen (736b35). Unsurprisingly, the male sex is the hotter of the two sexes, while the female has a cold nature. See D. M. Balme's notes to the Clarendon Press translation of *De Partibus Animalium* 1 and *De Generatione Animalium* 1 (1972). Balme suggests that the relation between vital heat and the *pneuma* is obscure (1972, 161–65).

30. Here it is difficult to miss the common resonance with Freud's infamous doctrine that woman is castrated. See Irigaray's famous critiques of Freud and Lacan in "The Blind Spot of an Old Dream of Symmetry" in S, 11–129/SA, 9–162.

31. Toril Moi's indictement of Irigaray's essentialism is one of the best known (985, 139). The divisive debate over essentialism in Irigaray's work is well handled by Chanter EE, 21–46. Also see Naomi Schor's important essay, "This Essentialism Which Is Not One" (1994).

32. "The question of the other has not been well formulated in the Western tradition, in which the other is always seen as the other of a singular subject and not an other subject" (Irigaray 2000, 123–4). This passage comes from an essay written thirty years after "How to Conceive of (a) Girl?" but Irigaray's position in the latter text is consistent with her first critique of Aristotle. Aristotle does not, of course, speak of the modern subject; nonetheless, his figurations of form and the other two masculine causes are congruent with the phallocentric representation of the male body, which is also implicit to thinking on subjectivity.

2. BEING IN PLACE

1. Irigaray's best readers acknowledge that "Place, Interval" and the introduction to *Ethics* are articulated in ontological terms. For example, see Olkowski RR, 83;

BI, 83; Deutscher ID, 107–22; Grosz and Cheah OBT, 3–18; Colebrook 1999a, 129–61; Farrell-Krell 1992, 306–14; Mortensen 2002, 87–97 and Diprose 1994, 36–37.

Chanter is the only commentator I know of to address Irigaray's specific motivations for reading Aristotle ontologically. Chanter has focused on Irigaray's "debt" to Heidegger's thinking on the meaning of being (EE, 146–51). Where Heidegger claims for Aristotle's elaboration of time in *Physics* 4.10–14 a foundational role in Western metaphysics, Irigaray "strategically" grants primordial status to Aristotle's theory of place. For Chanter, Irigaray is not doing fundamental ontology:

"Strategic because Irigaray is not making place foundational for space or space foundational for time . . . she is asking what it has meant, philosophically, to ground certain phenomena on others, who has been responsible for the hierarchies that are promulgated in such a process, and who has been excluded by such systematic thinking" (EE, 150).

In Chanter's reading, Irigaray turns to Aristotle's discussion of place in order to question the way in which woman has functioned as a provider of places for men—intrauterine places, sexual places, but the place of these places, that is woman herself, has remained unthought (EE, 158). Irigaray is particularly concerned with the way in which woman has functioned as the place of philosophy without having a place of her own. And there is no question that "Place, Interval" is articulated in relation to Heidegger's thinking on the meaning of Being, though I do not think Irigaray's interest in Aristotle's concept of place is merely a strategic response to Heidegger's attribution of foundational status to Aristotle's theory of time in *Physics* 4.10–14.

It falls beyond the aims of this book to trace the relationship between Irigaray's thinking on sexual difference and Heidegger's legacy. Briefly, though: for Irigaray, the primordial status of time in Heidegger is predicated on the appropriation of space. She spells this out in *The Forgetting of Air*. "Isn't time already an incorporation of space, whose tissue thus appropriated, will constitute subjectivity" (2000b, 95)? The tissue of space is the maternal-feminine (EE, 158; Irigaray 2000b, 95–96). Irigaray does not make space foundational for time; she is concerned with rethinking space *and* time. This is explicit in the introduction to *An Ethics of Sexual Difference*. "In order to live and think through . . . [sexual] difference, we must reconsider the whole question of *space* and *time*" (IR, 166; ESD, 7; E, 15). Irigaray's essay "Place, Interval" is one of the central works in which she engages in this immensely difficult task. For more on Irigaray's relationship to Heidegger, see Chanter EE, 127–69; Colebrook 1997; 1999a; Fielding 2003; Mortensen 1994, 211–46; 2002, 87–97; Joanna Hodge 1994, 199–209; Alison Ainley 1994; Stella Sanford 2001; Stone 2003; Faulkner 2001; and Farrell Krell 1992, 306–14.

2. Clarendon translation (1970).

3. Aristotle's well-known dispute with Plato on the question of space is a central intertext here. It falls beyond the scope of my intentions in this chapter to engage with Plato's discourse of *chōra* in the *Timaeus* (1961). Briefly, though: Aristotle reads *chōra* as geometrical space, which means it is unable to account for motion.

There is considerable debate about Aristotle's reading of Plato. Cornford warns against conflating *chōra* with geometrical space (1937, 177–8). Casey agrees with Cornford's position, while Algra and Duhem are sympathetic with Aristotle's critique of *chōra* (Casey 1998, 52–3; Algra 1995, 110–17; Duhem 1976b).

4. Bergson's early and little-known Latin thesis on the *Physics* contests Aristotle's theory of *topos* and supports the concept of infinitely divisible space on Kantian grounds. Bergson writes: "To those asking how can that exist which is devoid of quality and power and thus completely inactive, we reply that there are two modes of existence: one we call physical, that of an object composed of matter and form, the other mathematical, yet no less real, that of form separated from matter. We thus understand how our [modern] space is both empty and boundless. Aristotle is unable to concede this to us, nor would he wish to do so even if he could" (Bergson 1970, 67–68). Bergson's Latin thesis was first published in 1889, the same year as *Time and Free Will* (1913). From *Matter and Memory* (1981) onward, Bergson conceptualizes extensity in terms that are implicitly more sympathetic to Aristotle's anti-geometrism, although Bergson's conception of extensity diverges from Aristotle significantly.

5. The status of *topos* as something that surrounds a body will be complicated later. All quotations from *Physics* 4 are drawn from Hussey's Clarendon translation (1983b).

6. My reading of the sexed stakes of first *topos* conforms to the broad strokes of Irigaray's argument in "Place, Interval." But Irigaray's discussion of the distinction between common and first *topos* (what she calls proper place) takes up a different problematic than the one I address here. She pursues the questions of growth and of the relationship between matter and form (ESD, 36–37). These questions are of course bound up in the hierarchical sexuation of Aristotle's theory of *topos*, as we will see in the following chapter.

7. The sex of his students may be interesting historically but cannot serve as a justification of his masculinism. Such a justification is absurd given that Aristotle's work lives as written texts (in the phonocentric sense of the word *written*). His texts (and all texts) are capable of functioning in the absence of every determined addresser and addressee in general, so it is certainly possible for a woman to feel herself to be interpolated by Aristotle's *su*. Yet a woman, who does situate herself in this example, would be recuperated in phallocentrism, because the scenario is hierarchically sexed.

8. The Greek word *angeion* has a couple of senses that are explicitly associated with the maternal functions of woman's body. See Chapter Three.

9. From a Bergsonian perspective, a *diastēma* between musical notes is, at bottom, a measurable segment that is reducible to homogenous space. In this sense, Bergson would say the *diastēma* is a spatial concept that does not deal with the flow of real duration. See Chapter Four.

10. *A Greek–English Lexicon*, 8th ed., s.v. "diastēma."

11. See King, who draws Alexander of Aphrodisias' interpretation from Simplicius' *Corollaries of Place and Time* 583, 12–14, quoted by King (1950, 88–89); and Duhem in *Le System du Monde*, 1:200 quoted by King (1950, 88–89).

12. There are two paradoxes I have not addressed in the main body of my argument here. First, because a body must have something outside of it to be in place, the universe, which is the container par excellence, is not *en topōi*, because, in Aristotle's view, nothing is outside of the universe (212b16–21). So it is not only mobile bodies that escape the limits of *topos*; the universe is not surrounded by anything.

The second paradox has been developed at length by King (1950). Aristotle distinguishes between the situation in which something is potentially in place and a situation in which something is actually *en topōi* (212a31–b6; King 1950, 89–90). When the relations between the parts of a body are continuous, they are not actually in place, because they make up an organic whole. King proposes the example of a human eye. The retina, the nerves, the pupil, and so on form a single continuous body. Nonetheless, in Aristotle's terms, the parts of the eye are potentially *en topōi* because they *could* be divided (89–90). In contrast, something can be in place in actuality. Aristotle gives an example of this. When things are together, not continuously, but in direct contact, as in a heap, they are actually in place (212b5–6). The reason Aristotle says they are actually in place is that these bodies touch each other directly while remaining separable as individuals. The parts of an eye, on the other hand, are not distinct individuated entities but aspects of a continuous whole (*olon*).

For King, Aristotle's distinction between potential and actual place raises the question of where we demarcate between one body and another. This question, King notes, emerges because Aristotle conceives of all magnitude as continuous (219a11). Given that the sum of all magnitude is the universe, this means that the universe can be conceived as an organic whole (*olon*) (89–90). As King says, Aristotle does not solve the paradox of, on the one hand, demarcating between bodies that are merely contiguous and, on the other hand, of conceiving of all of a body as aspects of a continuous whole. The sense in which I am using the word "whole" (*olon*) here (i.e., as a continuous body made up of parts that form a single organic unity) sits in tension with Aristotle's use of "whole" (*olon*) to define the contiguous relation, between wine and jar, that I discussed earlier in this section. This tension is demonstrative of King's point: the distinction between one body and another is an unresolved paradox in Aristotle's thinking. Regardless of whether he resolved the status of the continuity of bodies, Aristotle, King argues, deserves praise, for he is the first thinker to raise as a problem the continuity of concrete extensity (91). Bergson's work on concrete extensity is remarkably close to King here. As I explain in Chapter Five, Bergson figures living reality as an enduring and evolving Whole.

King's essay is intellectually stimulating to read, but I am compelled to object to the extreme violence of his discourse. This is pronounced in his choice of example of potential place. His discussion of the potential to cut a human eye into pieces is violent in the worst sense of the word. King also makes prominent use of the phrase

"We murder to dissect" (94). He uses this phrase as a way of describing the move in his paper from critiquing Aristotle's concept of *topos* to positing an Aristotelian theory of space. His attraction to examples of cut-up bodies is all the more ironic given that his argument praises Aristotle as a thinker of continuity.

13. *A Greek–English Lexicon*, 8th ed., s.v. "en."

14. On Aristotle's struggle to refute otherness in excess of the categories, see Chapter One.

15. In chapter 3 of *Physics* 4, Aristotle uses the phrase "being in something else" (*estai en allōi*) in the same way that he uses the expression "a thing in something else" (*allo en allōi*) (210a25–34). The word *estai* is a conjugation of the Greek noun, *einai*, for being.

3. THE APORIA BETWEEN ENVELOPE AND THINGS

1. This is borne out by the extensive critical attention these texts have received. Scholars I know of who have engaged specifically with the radical formulation of nonhierarchical sexual difference that Irigaray elaborates in *An Ethics of Sexual Difference* include Casey 1998, 321–30; Chanter EE, 127–51; Colebrook 1999a; Deutscher ID, 107–22; Diprose, 1994, 36–7; Farrell Krell 1997, 159–74; Fielding 2003; Freeland 1999b; Grosz 1989, 173–8; 2001, 154–66; Olkowski 2000a, BI; Olkowski RR, 76–77; 80–88; Weiss 1999, 79–83; Whitford 1991, 149–68; and Ziarek 2001, 159–82.

2. Some key words in this aphorism deserve clarification. Irigaray's "*l'enveloppe*" and "*les choses*" are citations from Henri Carteron's French translation of the *Physics*. "*L'enveloppe*" translates one of the central concepts in Aristotle's definition of *topos*: *periechontos*. Hussey renders this important word as "that which surrounds" (212a20). "*Les choses*" refers to the various things that are in place. Aristotle alternates between two words to refer to the contained body, *allo* and *einai*. Thus, Irigaray's phrase "the relationship between envelope and things" should be read as a citation of Aristotle's conceptualization of bodies in place.

3. Chapter One discusses the disastrous implications of this. The conception of girl is rendered as a sort of monstrous aberration (S, 209/SA, 167).

4. *A Greek–English Lexicon*, 8th ed., s.v. "angeion."

5. In the interests of maintaining the important distinction between woman as the reassuring envelope of the man-embryo and the maternal-feminine as the disavowed outside of Aristotle's system, I have diverged from Irigaray's text here. She writes, "I shall affirm that the masculine is attracted to the maternal-feminine as place" (*je constaterai que le masculin est attiré vers le maternel-féminin comme lieu*) (ESD, 39/E, 45). While this is not faithful to the wording of her original text, I think my rendering is consistent with the broad strokes of Irigaray's critical description of Aristotle's phallocentrism.

6. Evelynn Hammonds addresses the complicity between the invisibility of Black women's sexuality in Western culture and the invisibility of black holes in

contemporary physics, in an essay entitled "Black (W)holes and the Geometry of Black Female Sexuality" (Hammonds 1994).

7. Of course, the word "cunt" is often used by men to insult each other. Think of the Australian cricketer, Darren Lehmann, who combined racism and misogyny by calling his Sri Lankan opponents "black cunts" when he was bowled out for a duck in a test match a few years ago. Many women use "cunt" as a term of abuse as well. I do not think this alters my argument. Women who use this word are spoken by phallocentrism, although their relation to "cunt" is different from a man's because this is a place they contain within themselves. In this sense, a woman who addresses another woman or a man as a "cunt" is also denigrating herself.

8. The womb, of course, is not immobile either, which makes it yet another example in which the distinction between *topos* and *angeion* collapses in Aristotle.

9. For another reading of the placenta as a modality of the interval related to the female body, see Gail M. Schwab's excellent essay "Mother's Body, Father's Tongue: Mediation and the Symbolic Order" (Schwab 1994).

10. Irigaray's interest in biological research on pregnancy demonstrates her commitment to engaging scientific discourses in a dialogue with philosophy. She is also critical of the phallocentrism(s) of the scientific tradition. See "Is the Subject of Science Sexed?" (Irigaray 1985a).

11. And perhaps, to flout the law of noncontradiction, the placenta should be affirmed as an ethical threshold *along with* the affirmation of a woman's right to abortion.

12. Peter Fenves develops a fascinating comparative reading of Irigaray's thinking on the mucus in relation to Walter Benjamin's influential essay "Toward a Critique of Violence." See Fenves 1998.

13. My modification of Burke and Gill's translation is partly derived from Casey's close reading of this passage in Irigaray (Casey 1997, 325). More generally, my reading of "Place, Interval" is indebted to Casey's subtle and sophisticated work on the same text.

14. This suggestion is partly inspired by a comment from Mary Beth Mader in her essay "All Too Familiar: Luce Irigaray's Recent Thought on Sexuation and Generation" (2003). Mader notes that in lovemaking women and men routinely enter each other's bodies (371). See my discussion of Mader in the main text of the following section.

15. See Judith Butler's well-known remarks in discussion with Cornell, Cheah, and Grosz in FSD, 27–28. The argument I offer in this section resonates closely with the position Grosz articulates in debate with Butler over Irigaray's alleged heterosexism. I agree with Grosz's assertion that Irigaray's work "has always been about addressing heterosexuality . . . she doesn't deal with homosexuality, hardly at all." The exception to this is Irigaray's essay "When the Goods Get Together" (TS, CS). Rather than consign Irigaray to what Butler calls "heterosexuality studies," I think it is more fruitful to pursue a question Grosz poses: "what would other relations of

sexuality be like if and when there was recognition of the existence of more than one sex?" (FSD, 28–29).

16. As we will see below, Mortensen is a notable exception to this tendency (2002, 7–19).

17. See Deutscher on the heterosociality of Irigaray's ethic of sexual difference (ID).

18. In the passage of *Sharing the World* under discussion, the interval is called "the approach" (Irigaray 2008, 35–36).

19. "Man re-creates woman outside, from inside-outside, he replaces himself outside, as an actor outside. . . . He reconstructs his body as a result of engendering the body of the other" (ESD 51/E, 55).

20. Freeland misconstrues this relationship. For Freeland, Irigaray's heterosexual erotics figure the sexes as "complementary wholes of form and matter" (1998b, 75). Sexual difference in the radical sense must be distinguished from complementarity, because it cannot allow for the fundamental openness that is central to Irigaray's formulation of the interval. Briefly: complementarity implies a relation in which each term fulfills or completes the other. On the entwinement of complementarity and phallocentrism, see Grosz 1989, 105.

21. Although Irigaray does invite man to rethink his morphology (TS, 135–36/CS, 133–34).

22. The rectum is acknowledged only in jokes and swearing. Think of straight-men's jokes about going to jail and getting "buggered." Or the popular (American?) swearword "arsehole"! And think of the figuration of man's mouth in advertising: it is either closed or protected by smiling white teeth. Woman's mouth, on the other hand, is frequently presented as a receptive opening, and often her mouth is shown with a phallic object "penetrating" it—fingers, icy poles, lollypops.

23. Mortensen develops this provocative argument as a critical response to the work of prominent feminist theorists, Butler and Rosi Braidotti. For Mortensen, both scholars recuperate phallocentrism in the very process of articulating female subjectivities. She suggests that these thinkers valorize dynamism and activity in highly phallocratic terms. "Might we not, in Butler's and Braidotti's theorising, have created a figure of female subjectivity that turns out to be [a] . . . phallic subject 'in drag'?" (2002, 15). This is all the more ironic for Mortensen, given that "such potency has long since ceased to be possible for any masculine, phallic subject in the age of modernity." Mortensen is writing here in the wake of Nietzsche's famous dictum "Man is dead."

24. One of the meanings the Greek word *angeion* ("woman" in Irigaray's account of Aristotle) is "sarcophagus" or "tomb." Her vagina-womb is paradoxically *topos*, in which both the beginnings of life and its dreaded end are entwined.

25. The acute phallocentric anxiety around the "penetrated" man is by no means peculiar to modernity and the era of AIDS. Michel Foucault emphasizes that "passivity" in men is highly problematic in ancient Greek culture as well. Where

the "passivity" of slaves or women poses no problems for the Greeks, a man who offers his body to be "penetrated" by another man is a figure of extreme difficulty. See Foucault 1987, 220.

26. This strikes me as a generous way to read Irigaray's normative claim that woman makes love within herself and man makes loves outside of himself (ESD, 51/E, 55–56). She is emphasizing the morphological irreducibility of experiencing carnal contact through a vagina and of experiencing carnality through a penis.

27. Aristotle shifts between *morphē* and *eidos* in his deduction of *physis* in *Physics* 2. *Morphē* is restricted to describing the form of *physis*, while *eidos* can be posited independently of *physis* (and *hylē*), as the very *ousia* of things.

28. In *I Love to You: Sketch of a Possible Felicity in History*, Irigaray specifically describes human nature as two. For instance, see chapter 2, "Human Nature Is Two." Alison Stone argues that Irigaray's conception of two irreducible natures emerges in her late works, particularly *Thinking the Difference* (1994), *I Love to You* (1996), and *To Be Two* (2000c). I disagree. The figuration of nature as two is necessarily implied in the way Irigaray radicalizes matter and form in *An Ethics of Sexual Difference*. I suspect that Stone misses Irigaray's transvaluative work on nature in *An Ethics of Sexual Difference* because Stone is inattentive to the interval. She describes the difference between male and female nature glibly as a "division" (Stone 2003).

29. Fielding's reading of Irigaray is very close to my position, although Fielding concentrates on Irigaray's transvaluation of Heidegger's reading of *physis*, while my argument is primarily concerned with Aristotle. Fielding is particularly attentive to the dynamic status of the interval. That said, I do not think that Irigaray's interval is as readily assimilable with Merleau-Ponty's chiasm as Fielding suggests in a deferential footnote to Olkowski (2000a). See Fielding 2003, 13, 25n29.

4. DUALISM IN BERGSON

1. Both Grosz and Olkowski relegate to footnotes their reservations about the phallic sexuation at play in Bergson. See Grosz NT, 291n6 and Olkowski RR, 278n98.

2. Aristotle distinguishes hierarchically between different forms of knowledge. The lowest form is sense perception, of which both animals and humans are capable. The knowledge of creatures able to generate memory from sense data occupies the next level in Aristotle's hierarchy. This is not sufficient to constitute proper experience. For Aristotle, only "men" are capable of connected experience, which is the third kind of knowledge. This, in turn, enables various rules of practice. Use of these rules to make things without understanding the principles on which they depend is a still more privileged form of knowledge. Above the use of rules of practice is "art" (*technē*), which involves understanding the general principles that underpin the rules of practice. The supreme form of knowledge is metaphysics, the science of elaborating general principles of universals. Unlike all other forms of knowledge, metaphysics exists for itself. (980a22–982a2). See also, Ross 1964, 154.

3. This is not to suggest that intellect is an exclusively human instrument of action. For Bergson the most important characteristics of intellect are language, the making of tools, and the use of homogeneous space and time. As is well known, a number of primate species make use of tools to feed themselves, and domesticated dogs readily learn to understand up to two hundred spoken words.

4. Marie Cariou suggests that Bergson's critique of the paradoxes misconstrues Zeno's position. She argues that Zeno reasons from absurdity without affirming the absurdities as his own. For Cariou, Bergson misses Zeno's irony: "Zeno was probably more Bergsonian than Bergson thought" (NB, 111). I am inclined to think Bergson's relation to Zeno is more ambiguous than Cariou allows. On the one hand, as she argues, Zeno is faulted for failing to consider real movement (MM, 191/O, 327). On the other hand, Bergson clearly admires his acute diagnosis of the impossibility of understanding movement as the intellect represents it. For Bergson, the paradoxes confirm the masking of duration by making manifest the necessary contradictions generated by translating movement into symbols conceived in intellectual space. Bergson returns to Zeno's paradoxes throughout his work because they bring out these contradictions so clearly. This does not necessarily mean, as Cariou contends, that Bergson takes Zeno literally to affirm the absurdities. In my view, Bergson's criticism is focused on the absence in Zeno's postulates of an alternative theory that avoids the contradictions of reducing motion to a series of points in space. Of course, it is contrary to the classical form of the paradox to provide a positive theory of motion. But Bergson is more interested in philosophy becoming a discipline that understands the novelty of becoming than he is in respecting the aporetic conventions of classical antinomies.

Bergson discusses Zeno's paradoxes throughout his career. See TFW, 112–14/O, 74–77; MM, 191–93, 258n2/O, 326–29; CE, 308–14/O, 755–60; CM, 17–18/O, 1258–59; and 1977, 73/O, 1036–37.

5. See Chapter Two for an analysis of Aristotle's preference for place (*topos*) over space (*chōra*).

6. These comments are drawn from a close reading of the passage that serves as the epigraph of this chapter (CM, 12/O, 1254–5).

7. Kant says that the schema of magnitude as a concept of the understanding is number. Number "comprises the successive addition of homogeneous units. Number is therefore simply the unity of the synthesis of the manifold of a homogeneous intuition in general, a unity due to my generating time itself in the apprehension of the intuition" (Kant 1976, 183–84, B182). For Roland Breeur, "the real key (and this is often forgotten) to his [Bergson's] critique of the contamination of time by space (and of a conception of a 'homogeneous time') is, strikingly, Kant's schematism, and more precisely Kant's category for the schematism of magnitude [*Grosse*]." Breeur suggests that Bergson's critique in *Time and Free Will* is done in a kind of fidelity to the Kantian conviction that time is a form of inner sense. The time of Kant "was probably only masked space; but thanks to his 'critique of the critique',

Bergson opens a route to originary, non-contaminated time, and thus to 'real' interiority." See Breeur 2001, 179–80.

8. In the second chapter of *Creative Evolution*, Bergson establishes a difference in nature between instinct, which reaches its most sophisticated form in insects, and intelligence, which has evolved to its greatest complexity in the human species. This has received a lot of critical attention. See Deleuze B, 108, 110/BE, 113–14, 117; Mullarkey BP, 78–80, 158–60; Ansell-Pearson GL, 50–52; and especially H. Wildon Carr 1919, 31–44.

9. It is not clear to me how the reader of a text by a writer long dead could stir me to vibrate in unison with his or her mind, unless we accept Bergson's more hypothetical suggestions found in his late work that mind may be immortal. Could I by intuitive reading invoke the spirit of Bergson? Is that what he is suggesting? On the immortality of mind, see ME, 35–36/O, 835–36.

10. Isn't this just what Derrida has called the powerful, irrepressible desire for a transcendental signified? Famously, for Derrida, this tendency recurs throughout the history of metaphysics (1974, 11–12; 1981, 19–20).

11. See also see Lawlor 2004, 28, 38.

12. This monistic conception of life is by no means peculiar to the Nunga. For example, for the Warlpiri, Tanganekald, Meintangk, and Quandamooka peoples, the traditional Western demarcations between subject and object, between land and people, and between nature, culture, and subject do not operate (Langton 1993, Watson 2002a, 2002b, Moreton-Robinson 2002).

5. INTERVAL, SEXUAL DIFFERENCE

1. Olkowski's reading of Bergson and Irigaray effectively points out the fundamental importance of the interval to their respective projects, but Olkowski (RR, 80–83; BI) does not address the divergences between Irigaray and Bergson. Grosz does not offer a detailed account of the relationship between Bergsonian qualitative difference (what I call the interval) and the Irigarayan interval of sexual difference. Like Olkowski though, Grosz affirms a strong affinity between Bergson and Irigaray. In the introduction to *The Nick of Time*, Grosz suggests that Irigaray's project "develops, perhaps more than any other writer since Bergson, a practical metaphysics that rigorously develops Bergsonian intuition as its primary method" (NT, 14). I disagree. The relationship between Irigaray's approach to the question of sexual difference and Bergsonian intuition is more fraught than Grosz suggests here.

2. In conversation, Paul Atkinson suggested to me that Bergson's conception of consciousness as duration depends upon a distinction between the inside and the outside of the self—a spatial difference. Without maintaining this intellectual distinction, Bergson could not posit an inner life as such.

3. For instance, see Genevieve Lloyd 1984.

4. "En un mot, si l'on convient d'appeler libre tout acte qui émane du moi, et du moi seulement, l'acte qui porte la marque de notre personne est véritablement libre, car notre moi seul en revendiquera la paternité" (O, 114).

5. He praises woman's incomparable supra-intellectual ability as a mother. Bergson's praise is directed toward the mother's role as the nurturer of her child rather than as her child's creator.

6. The presentation of consciousness or thought as a self-originating act of fathering is by no means novel in metaphysics. Irigaray's famous reading of Plato's parable of the cave devotes a great deal of attention to the presentation of the birth of the intelligible Forms in exclusively paternal terms. She argues that the gesture of crediting the father as sole creator of his offspring is achieved only on condition that the maternal-feminine serves as the silenced ground of Plato's theoretical elaboration (Irigaray S, 243–364/SA, 301–457). Of course, the emphasis of Bergson's thought experiment on duration has little in common with the eternal forms of Plato. Nonetheless, both philosophers elide the maternal-feminine and posit metaphysics as monosexual. Deleuze notes Bergson's strong attachment to Platonic metaphors (Deleuze B, 44–45/BE, 39).

6. BEYOND MAN: RETHINKING LIFE AND MATTER

1. Humanism and phallocentrism are not reducible, because it is possible to exceed phallocentrism and remain bound up in anthropocentrism. As I argue in the following chapter, Irigaray's work can be read as anthropocentric because of her habit of construing sexual difference as the decisive difference between human beings. Posthumanism, if there is such a thing, must exceed phallocentrism, for traces of the phallic are necessarily traces of the privilege of "Man."

2. William E. May argues that the limit of pure freedom described in this passage is how Bergson conceives of God (May 1970, 637).

3. It is only in his first book, *Time and Free Will*, that Bergson identifies matter with pure space. In all of his subsequent publications, the absolute passivity sketched in this passage is a pure limit beyond the actual. See May 1970, 614–15.

4. In this instance, Bergson defines materiality, without qualification, as *pure* repetition. In the passages from *The Creative Evolution* I have just discussed, Bergson says matter stops short of *pure* repetition. The passage comes from his important essay "An Introduction to Metaphysics" (CM, 159–200), which was published several years after *Matter and Memory* but before *The Creative Evolution*.

5. Bergson refers to "sexuality" in the first chapter of *The Creative Evolution*. He also makes a few references to sex cells (CE, 59–60, 79–80/O, 545–46, 563–64). The neglect of this primitive differentiation is even more marked in Deleuze's reading of *The Creative Evolution*. Deleuze provides a diagram summarizing the divergence of the *élan vital* into distinct actualities and omits what Bergson calls "sexual generation" (B, 102/BE, 106).

6. It is perhaps unfair to chastise Bergson for neglecting to mention the egg in this image. After all, the active part played by ovum in the selection of sperm to create an embryo was not discovered until the second half of the twentieth century.

7. Bergson speculates that the mind may outlive the body. Living in the conventional sense may prepare consciousness for "more efficient action, an intenser life," no longer harnessed to the matter of the body (ME, 35/O, 835).

8. Bergson uses "consciousness" and "life" interchangeably here.

9. Bergson also identifies the complexity of the human brain, social life, and languages in his argument for Man's superiority over other life forms on this planet (CE, 264–65/O, 719–20).

10. I found that De Landa's discussion of the scientific background to Deleuze's conception of multiplicity is a particularly valuable contribution to this field. See especially chapter 1, "The Mathematics of the Virtual: Manifolds, Vector Field and Transformation Groups" (De Landa 2002, 9–55).

CONCLUSION: INTERVAL AS RELATION, INTERVAL AS BECOMING

1. In conversation, Jami Weinstein suggested that Irigaray would refuse my reading of her formulation of sexual difference. For Weinstein, my emphasis on Irigaray's use of the "perhaps" draws out a minor tendency in Irigaray that runs counter to her major position in which sexual difference is figured as primary without qualification.

BIBLIOGRAPHY

Adkins, A. W. H. (1970). *From the Many to the One*. London: Constable.

Agamben, Giorgio. (1999). *Potentialities: Collected Essays in Philosophy*. Translated by Daniel Heller-Roazen. Stanford: Stanford University Press.

Ainley, Alison. (1995). "Luce Irigaray: At Home with Martin Heidegger?" *Angelaki* 2 (1): 139–45.

Algra, Keimpe. (1995). *Concepts of Space in Greek Thought*. Philosophia Antiqua A Series of Studies on Ancient Philosophy 65. Leiden: E. J. Brill.

"Allo." (1996). *A Greek–English Lexicon*. 8th ed.

"Angeion." (1996). *A Greek–English Lexicon*. 8th ed.

Ansell-Pearson, Keith. (1999a). *Germinal Life: The Difference and Repetition of Deleuze*. London: Routledge.

———. (1999b). Bergson and Creative Evolution/Involution: Exposing the Transcendental Illusion of Organismic Life. In *The New Bergson*, edited by John Mullarkey. Manchester: Manchester University Press.

———. (2002). *Philosophy and the Adventure of the Virtual: Bergson and the Time of Life*. London: Routledge.

Aquinas, St. Thomas. (1963). *Commentary on Aristotle's Physics*. Translated by R. Blackwell, R. Spath and, W. Thirlkel. New Haven: Yale University Press.

Aristotle. (1933). *The Metaphysics I–IX*. Translated by Hugh Tredennick. London: William Heineman.

———. (1935). *The Metaphysics X–XIV*. Translated by Hugh Tredennick. 2nd ed. Cambridge, Mass.: Harvard University Press.

———. (1936). *Aristotle's Physics*. Text and commentrary by W. D. Ross. Oxford: Clarendon.

———. (1953). *The Generation of Animals*. Translated by A. L. Peck. Cambridge, Mass.: Harvard University Press.

———. (1961). *Physique I–IV*. Translated by Henri Carteron. Volume 1. Paris: Budé.

———. (1966). *De l'Ame* Translated by A. Jannone. Paris: Budé.

———. (1970). *Aristotle's Physics I and II*. Translated by William Charlton. Oxford: Clarendon.

———. (1972). *Aristotle's De Partibus Animalium I and Generatione Animalium I*. Translated by D. M. Balme. Oxford: Clarendon.

———. (1983a). *Aristotle's De Anima, Books II, III*. Translated by D. W. Hamlyn. Oxford: Clarendon.

———. (1983b). *Aristotle's Physics: Books III and IV*. Translated by Edward Hussey. Oxford: Clarendon.

———. (1984). *The Complete Works of Aristotle*. Edited by Jonathan Barnes. 2 vols. Revised translation. Princeton: Princeton University Press.

———. (1985). *Metaphysics*. Translated by Montgomery Furth. Indianapolis: Hackett.

———. (1993). *Aristotle's Metaphysics: Books G, D, and E*. Translated by Christopher Kirwan. 2nd ed. Oxford: Clarendon.

Atterton, Peter, and Mathew Calarco, eds. (2004). *Animal Philosophy*. London: Continuum.

Bachelard, Gaston. (2000). *The Dialectic of Duration*. Translated by Mary McAllister Jones. Manchester: Clinamen.

Barden, Garrett. (1999). "Method in Philosophy." In *The New Bergson*, edited by John Mullarkey. Manchester: Manchester University Press.

Bar On, Bat Ami. (1994). *Engendering Origins: Critical Feminist Readings in Plato and Aristotle*. Albany: State University of New York Press.

Bennington, Geoffrey, and Jacques Derrida. (1993). *Jacques Derrida*. Translated by Geoffrey Bennington. Chicago: University of Chicago Press.

Benjamin, Walter. (1973). *Illuminations*. Translated by Harry Zohn. Edited by Hannah Arendt. London: Fontana.

Bergson, Henri. (1913). *Time and Free Will: An Essay on the Immediate Data of Consciousness*. Translated by F. L. Pogson. London: George Allen.

———. (1920). *Mind-Energy*. Translated by H. Wildon Carr. New York: Henry Holt.

———. (1959). *Œuvres*. Paris: Presses Universitaires de France.

———. (1970). "Aristotle's Concept of Place." Translated by John K. Ryan. In *Studies in Philosophy and the History of Philosophy*. Volume 5, *Ancients and Moderns*. Washington, D.C.: Catholic University of America Press. 20–72.

———. (1972). *Mélanges*. Edited by André Robinet. Paris: Presses Universitaires de France.

———. (1977). *The Two Sources of Morality and Religion*. Translated by R. Ashley Audra and Cloudsley Brereton. Notre Dame, Ind.: University of Notre Dame Press.

———. (1983). *Creative Evolution*. Translated by Arthur Mitchell. Lanham, Md.: University Press of America.

———. (1981). *Matter and Memory*. Translated by Nancy Margaret Paul and W. Scott Palmer. New York: Zone.

———. (1992). *The Creative Mind An Introduction to Metaphysics*. Translated by Mabelle L. Andison. New York: Citadel.

———. (1999). "A letter from Bergson to John Dewey." Translated by Ryu Jiseok. In *The New Bergson*, edited by John Mullarkey. Manchester: Manchester University Press.

———. (2002). *Henri Bergson: Key Writings*. Edited by Keith Ansell Pearson and John Mullarkey. New York: Continuum.

Bersani, Leo. (1987). "Is the Rectum a Grave?" In *AIDS: Cultural Analysis, Cultural Criticism*, edited by Douglas Crimp. Cambridge, Mass.: MIT Press.

Boundas, Constantin. (1996). "Deleuze–Bergson: An Ontology of the Virtual." In *Deleuze: A Critical Reader*, edited by Paul Patton. Oxford: Blackwell.

Brentano, Franz. (1975). *On the Several Senses of Being in Aristotle*. Translated by Rolf George. Berkeley: University of California Press.

———. (1978). *Aristotle and His World View*. Translated and edited by Rolf George and Roderick M. Chisholm. Berkeley: University of California Press.

Burke, Carolyn, Naomi Schor, and Margaret Whitford, eds. (1994). *Engaging with Irigaray: Feminist Philosophy and Modern European Thought*. New York: Columbia University Press.

Butler, Judith. (1993). *Bodies That Matter: On the Discursive Limits of "Sex."* New York: Routledge.

Butler, Judith, Drucilla Cornell, with Pheng Cheah, and Elizabeth Grosz. (1998). "The Future of Sexual Difference: An Interview with Judith Butler and Drucilla Cornell." *Diacritics* 28 (1): 19–42.

Cadava, Eduardo, Peter Connor, and Jean-Luc Nancy, eds. (1991). *Who Comes after the Subject?* New York: Routledge.

Capek, Milic. (1961). "The Elusive Nature of the Past." In *Experience, Existence, and the Good: Essays in Honor of Paul Weiss*, edited by Irwin C. Lieb. Carbondale: Southern Illinois University Press.

———. (1969). "Bergson's Theory of Matter and Modern Physics." In *Bergson and the Evolution of Physics*, edited by P. A. Y. Gunter. Knoxville: University of Tennessee Press.

———. (1971). *Bergson and Modern Physics: A Reinterpretation and Re-evaluation*. Dordrecht: Nijhoff.

Cariou, Marie. (1999). "The Keyboards of Forgetting." Translated by Melissa McMahon. In *The New Bergson*, edited by John Mullarkey. Manchester: Manchester University Press.

Carr, H. Wildon. (1919). *Henri Bergson: The Philosophy of Change*. London: T. C. and E. C. Jack.

Caruth, Cathy. (1996). *Unclaimed Experience: Trauma, Narrative and History*. Baltimore: Johns Hopkins University Press.

Casey, Edward S. (1997). *The Fate of Place: A Philosophical History*. Berkeley: University of California Press.

Chanter, Tina. (1995). *Ethics of Eros: Irigaray's Rewriting of the Philosophers*. New York: Routledge.

Charlton, William. (1970). Introduction to *Aristotle's Physics I and II*. Oxford: Clarendon.

Cheah, Pheng. (1996). "Mattering." *Diacritics* 26 (1): 108–39.

Cheah, Pheng, and Elizabeth Grosz, eds. (1998). "The Political Future of Sexual Difference." Special issue, *Diacritics* 28 (1).

———. (1998). "Of Being-Two: Introduction." *Diacritics* 28 (1): 3–18.

Colebrook, Claire. (1997). "Feminist Philosophy and the Philosophy of Feminism: Irigaray and the History of Western Metaphysics." *Hypatia* 12 (1): 79–98.

———. (1999a). *Ethics and Representation: From Kant to Post-structuralism*. Edinburgh: Edinburgh University Press.

———. (1999b). "Is Sexual Difference a Problem?" In *Deleuze and Feminist Theory*, edited by Claire Colebrook and Ian Buchanan. Edinburgh: Edinburgh University Press.

———. (2001). "Passive Synthesis and Life." Parallax 7 (4): 9–28.

———. (2008). Introduction: I. "Deleuze and Gender," edited by Claire Colebrook and Jami Weinstein. Special issue, *Deleuze Studies* 2 (supplement): 1–19

Colebrook, Claire, and Jami Weinstein, eds. (2008). "Deleuze and Gender." Special issue, Deleuze Studies 2 (supplement).

Cornford, Francis MacDonald. (1932). *Before and after Socrates*. Cambridge: Cambridge University Press.

———. (1952). *Principium Sapientiae: A Study of the Origins of Greek Philosophical Thought*. New York: Harper and Row.

———, trans. (1937). *Plato's Cosmology: The Timaeus of Plato: Translated, with a Running Commentary by Francis MacDonald Cornford*. London: Kegan Paul.

Crary, Jonathan, and Sanford Kwinter, eds. (1992). *Incorporations*. Zone 6. New York: Zone.

Darwin, Charles. (1968). *The Origin of Species*. Harmondsworth: Penguin.

Dastur, Françoise. (1992). "The Ekstatico-Horizonal Constitution of Temporality." In *Martin Heidegger: Critical Assessments*, edited by Christopher Macann. Volume 1. London: Routledge.

Davies, Paul and John Gribbin. (1992). *The Matter Myth: Beyond Chaos and Complexity*. London: Penguin.

de Landa, Manuel. (1992). Nonorganic Life. In *Incorporations*. Zone 6. Edited by Jonathan Crary and Sanford Kwinter. New York: Zone.

———. (2002). *Intensive Science and Virtual Philosophy*. London: Continuum.

Deleuze, Gilles. (1968). *Le Bergsonisme*. Paris: Presses Universitaire de France.

———. (1984). *Kant's Critical Philosophy: The Doctrine of the Faculties*. Translated by Hugh Tomlinson and Barbara Habberjam. London: Athlone.

———. (1988). *Foucault*. Translated and edited by Seán Hand. Minneapolis: University of Minnesota Press.

———. (1991). *Bergsonism*. Translated by Hugh Tomlinson and Barbara Habberjam. New York: Zone.

———. (1994). *Difference and Repetition*. Translated by Paul Patton. New York: Columbia University Press.

———. (1997). *Essays: Critical and Clinical*. Translated by Daniel W. Smith and Michael A. Greco. Minneapolis: Minnesota University Press.

———. (1999). "Bergson's Conception of Difference." Translated by Melissa McMahon. In *The New Bergson*, edited by John Mullarkey. Manchester: Manchester University Press.

———. (2002). "Description of Woman: For a Philosophy of the Sexed Other." Translated by Keith W. Faulkner. *Angelaki*. 7 (3): 17–24.

Deleuze, Gilles, and Felix Guattari. (1987). *A Thousand Plateaus: Capitalism and Schizophrenia*. Translated by Brian Massumi. Minneapolis: Minnesota University Press.

Delhomme, Jeanne. (1954). *Vie et conscience de la vie*. Paris: Presses Universitaire de France.

Derrida, Jacques. (1974). *Of Grammatology*. Translated by Gayatri Chakravorty Spivak. Baltimore: Johns Hopkins University Press.

———. (1981). *Positions*. Translated by Alan Bass. Chicago: Chicago University Press.

———. (1982). *Margins of Philosophy*. Translated by Alan Bass. Chicago: Chicago University Press.

———. (1983). "Geschlect. Sexual Difference, Ontological Difference." Translated by Rubin Berezdin. *Research in Phenomenology* 13: 65–83.

———. (1985). *The Ear of the Other: Otobiography, Transference, Translation*. Translated by Avital Ronell. New York: Schocken Books.

———. (1989). "Women in the Beehive." In *Men in Feminism*, edited by Alice Jardine and Paul Smith. New York: Routledge.

———. (1993). *Aporias*. Translated by Thomas Dutoit. Stanford: Stanford University Press.

———. (1995). "Khora." In *On the Name*, translated by David Wood, John P. Leavey Jr., and Ian McLeod. Stanford: Stanford University Press.

———. (1997). *Politics of Friendship*. Translated by George Collins. London: Verso.

———. (2004). This Animal that Therefore I Am. Translated by David Wills. In *Animal Philosophy*. Edited by Mathew Calarco and Peter Atterton. London: Continuum.

Descombes, Vincent. (1980). *Modern French Philosophy*. Translated by L. Scott-Fox and J. M. Harding. Cambridge: Cambridge University Press.

Deslauriers, Marguerite. (1999). "Sex and Essence in Aristotle's *Metaphysics* and Biology." In *Feminist Interpretations of Aristotle*, edited by Cynthia A. Freeland. University Park: Pennsylvania State University Press.

Deutscher, Penelope. (2002). *A Politics of Impossible Difference: The Later Work of Luce Irigaray*. Ithaca, N.Y.: Cornell University Press.

"Diarao." (1996). *A Greek–English Lexicon*. 8th ed.

"Diastēma." (1996). *A Greek–English Lexicon*. 8th ed.

Diprose, Rosalyn. (1994). *The Bodies of Women: Ethics, Embodiment, and Sexual Difference*. London: Routledge.

Duhem, Pierre. (1976a). "Plato's Theory of Space and the Geometrical Composition of the Elements." Translated by David A. Sipfle and Mary-Alice Sipfle. In *The Concepts of Space and Time: Their Structure and Development*, edited by Milic Capek. Boston Studies in the Philosophy of Science 22. Dordrecht: D. Reidel.

———. (1976b). "Space and Void According to Aristotle." Translated by David A. Sipfle and Mary-Alice Sipfle. In *The Concepts of Space and Time: Their Structure and Development*, edited by Milic Capek. Boston Studies in the Philosophy of Science 22. Dordrecht: D. Reidel.

"En." (1996). *A Greek–English Lexicon*. 8th ed.

Fanon, Frantz. (1967). *Black Skin, White Masks*. Translated by Charles Lam Markmann. New York: Grove.

Faulkner, Joanne. (2001). "Amnesia at the Beginning of Time: Irigaray's Reading of Heidegger in *The Forgetting of Air*." *Contretemps* 2: 124–41.

Fenves, Peter. (1998). "Out of the Order of Number: Benjamin and Irigaray Toward a Politics of Pure Means." *Diacritics* 28 (1): 43–58.

Feyman, Richard P. (1998). *Six Easy Pieces: The Fundamentals of Physics Explained*. London: Penguin.

Fielding, Helen. (2003). "Irigaray, Heidegger, and the Potentiality of Matter." *Continental Philosophy Review* 36 (1): 1–26.

Foucault, Michel. (1979). *The History of Sexuality.* Volume 1, *An Introduction*. Translated by Robert Hurley. London: Allen Lane.

———. (1980). *Power/Knowledge: Selected Interviews and Other Writins, 1972–1977*. Edited by Colin Gordon. Translated by Colin Gordon, Leo Marshall, John Mepham, and Kate Sopher. New York: Pantheon.

———. (1987). *The History of Sexuality.* Volume 2, *The Use of Pleasure*. Translated by Robert Hurley. London: Penguin.

Freeland, Cynthia, ed. (1999a). *Feminist Interpretations of Aristotle*. University Park: Pennsylvania State University Press.

———. (1999b). "On Irigaray on Aristotle." In *Feminist Interpretations of Aristotle*, edited by Cynthia A. Freeland. University Park: Pennsylvania State University Press.

Freeman, Kathleen, ed. (1957). *Ancilla to the Pre-Socratic Philosophers*. Translated by Kathleen Freeman. Cambridge, Mass: Harvard University Press.

———. (1966). *The Pre-Socratic Philosophers*. Oxford: Basil Blackwood.

Freud, Sigmund. (1985). Civilization and Its Discontents. Edited and translated by James Strachey and Angela Richards. Penguin Freud Library 12. London: Penguin.

———. (1962). "Femininity." Translated by James Strachey. Edited by James Strachey and Angela Richards. Penguin Freud Library 2. London: Penguin.

Furley, David J. (1976). "Aristotle and the Atomists on Motion in a Void." In *Motion and Time Space and Matter*, edited by Peter K. Machamer and Robert G. Turnbull. Columbus: Ohio State University Press.

Gatens, Moira. (1996). *Imaginary Bodies: Ethics, Power, and Corporeality*. London: Routledge.

Garcia-Duttman, Alexander. (2000). "A Short Diary of the New." Translated by Humphrey Bower. In *Small Acts: Performance, the Millennium and the Marking of Time*, edited by Adrian Heathfield. London: Black Dog.

Granger, Herbert. (1984). "Aristotle on Genus and Differentia." *Journal of the History of Philosophy* 22 (1): 1–23.

Grisoni, Dominique. (1989). "Onomatopoeia of Desire." Translated by Paul Foss. *Theoretical Strategies*, edited by Peter Botsman. Sydney: Local Consumption Publications.

Grosz, Elizabeth. (1989). *Sexual Subversions: Three French Feminists*. Sydney: Allen and Unwin.

———. (1994). *Volatile Bodies: Toward a Corporeal Feminism*. Sydney: Allen and Unwin.

———. (1995). *Space, Time, and Perversion*. Sydney: Allen and Unwin.

———, ed. (1999a). *Becomings: Explorations in Time Memory and Futures*. Ithaca, N.Y.: Cornell University Press.

———. (1999b). "Deleuze's Bergson: Duration, the Virtual and a Politics of the Future." In *Deleuze and Feminist Theory*, edited by Claire Colebrook and Ian Buchanan. Edinburgh: Edinburgh University Press.

———. (2001). *Architecture from the Outside: Essays on Virtual and Real Space*. Cambridge, Mass.: MIT Press.

———. (2002). "The Politics of the Same in Science: Feminist Science?" Unpublished paper.

———. (2004). *The Nick of Time: Politics, Evolution, and the Untimely*. Sydney: Allen and Unwin.

———. (2005). *Time Travels: Feminism, Nature, Power*. Sydney: Allen and Unwin.

Gunter, P. A. Y., ed. (1969). *Bergson and the Evolution of Physics*. Knoxville: University of Tennessee Press.

Gunter, P. A. Y., and Ander C. Papanicolaou, eds. (1987). *Bergson and Modern Thought*. New York: Harwood.

Guthrie, W. K. (1981). *A History of Greek Philosophy*. Volume 6, *Aristotle, an Encounter*. Cambridge: Cambridge University Press.

Hammonds, Evelynn. (1994). "Black (W)holes and the Geometry of Black Female Sexuality." *Differences: A Journal of Feminist Cultural Studies* 6 (2.3): 126–45.

Hanna, Thomas, ed. (1962). *The Bergsonian Heritage*. New York: Columbia University Press.

Hawking, Stephen. (1988). *A Brief History of Time: From the Big Bang to Black Holes*. Toronto: Bantam.

Heidegger, Martin. (1969). *Identity and Difference*. Translated by Joan Stambaugh. New York: Harper and Row.

———. (1993). *Basic Works*. Edited by David Farrell Krell. London: Routledge.

———. (1998). "On the Essence and Concept of Physis in Aristotle's Physics B, 1." Translated by Thomas Sheehan. In *Pathmarks*, edited by William McNeill. Cambridge: Cambridge University Press.

Herodotus. (1972). *The Histories*. Translated by Aubrey de Sélincourt. Harmondsworth: Penguin.

Hesiod. (1988). *Theogony and Works and Days*. Translated by M. L. West. Oxford: Oxford University Press.

Hill, Rebecca. (2008a). "Interval, Sexual Difference: Luce Irigaray and Henri Bergson." *Hypatia* 23 (1): 119–31.

———. (2008b). "Phallocentrism in Bergson: Life and Matter." *Deleuze Studies* 2 (supplement): 20–33.

Hirsch, Elizabeth, and Gary A. Olson. (1995). "'Je—Luce Irigaray': A Meeting with Luce Irigaray." *Hypatia* 10(2): 93–114.

Hodge, Joanna. (1994). "Irigaray Reading Heidegger." In *Engaging with Irigaray: Feminist Philosophy and Modern European Thought*, edited by Carolyn Burke, Naomi Schor, and Margaret Whitford. New York: Columbia University Press.

Hussey, Edward. (1983). Introduction to *Aristotle's Physics: Books III and IV*. Oxford: Clarendon.

"Hylē." (1996). *A Greek–English Lexicon*. 8th ed.

"Interval." (1989). *The Oxford English Dictionary*. 2nd ed.

"Intervalle." (1993). *Nouveau petit Robert dictionnaire de la langue française*.

Irigaray, Luce. (1974). *Speculum de l'autre femme*. Paris: Minuit.

———. (1977). *Ce sexe qui n'en est pas un*. Paris: Minuit.

———. (1981). "Women's Exile." *Ideology and Consciousness*, 1: 62–76.

———. (1982). *Passions élémentaires*. Paris: Minuit.

———. (1984). *Éthique de la différence sexuelle*. Paris: Minuit.

———. (1985a). "Is the Subject of Science Sexed?" Translated by Edith Oberle. *Cultural Critique* 1: 73–88.

———. (1985b). *Speculum of the Other Woman*. Translated by Gillian C. Gill. Ithaca: Cornell University Press.

———. (1985c). *This Sex Which Is Not One*. Translated by Catherine Porter with Carolyn Burke. Ithaca: Cornell University Press.

———. (1991a). *The Irigaray Reader*. Edited by Margaret Whitford. Oxford: Blackwell.

———. (1991b). *Marine Lover of Friedrich Nietzsche*. Translated by Gillian C. Gill. New York: Columbia University Press.

———. (1992). *Elemental Passions*. Translated by Joanne Collie and Judith Still. New York: Routledge.

———. (1993a). *An Ethics of Sexual Difference*. Translated by Carolyn Burke and Gillian C. Gill. Ithaca: Cornell University Press.

———. (1993b). *Je, Tu, Nous: Toward a Culture of Difference*. Translated by Alison Martin. New York: Routledge.

———. (1993c). *Sexes and Genealogies*. Translated by Gillian C. Gill. New York: Columbia University Press.

———. (1994). *Thinking the Difference: For a Peaceful Revolution*. Translated by Karin Montin. London: Althone.

———. (1996). *I Love to You: Sketch of a Possible Felicity in History*. Translated by Alison Martin. New York: Routledge.

———. (2000a). *Democracy Begins between Two*. Translated by Kirsteen Anderson. London: Althone.

———. (2000b). *The Forgetting of Air*. Translated by Mary Beth Mader. Austin: University of Texas Press.

———. (2000c). *To Be Two*. Translated by Monique M. Rhodes and Marco F. Cocito-Monoc. London: Althone.

———. (2000d). *Why Different?A Culture of Two Subjects*. Edited by Luce Irigaray and Sylvère Lotringer. Translated by Camille Collins. New York: Semiotext(e).

———. (2002a). *Between East and West: From Singularity to Community*. Translated by Stephen Pluháček. New York: Columbia.

———. (2002b). *To Speak Is Never Neutral*. Translated by Gail Schwab. London: Continuum.

———. (2002c). *The Way of Love*. Translated by Heidi Bostic and Stephen Pluháček. London: Continuum.

———. (2004a). *Luce Irigaray: Key Writings*. Edited by Luce Irigaray. London: Continuum.

———. (2004b). "Animal Compassion." Translated by Marilyn Gaddis Rose. In *Animal Philosophy: Essential Reading in Continental Thought*, edited by Matthew Calarco and Peter Atterton. London: Continuum.

———. (2008). *Sharing the World*. Translated by Stephen Pluháček. London: Continuum.

Itzkowitz, Kenneth. (1982). "Reaching Beyond Aristotle: A Note on Absolute or Ontological Difference." *The New Scholasticism* 56: 340–45.

James, William. (1977). *A Pluralistic Universe*. Cambridge, Mass.: Harvard University Press.

Jankelevitch, Vladimir. (1959). *Henri Bergson*. Paris: Presses Universitaires de France.

Jay, Nancy. (1981). "Gender and Dichotomy." *Feminist Studies* 1: 38–56.

Johnson, Barbara. (1996). "Muteness Envy." In *Human, All Too Human*, edited by Diana Fuss. New York: Routledge.

Kant, Immanuel. (1929). *Immanuel Kant's Critique of Pure Reason*. Translated by Norman Kemp Smith. London: Macmillan.

Kearney, Richard, and Emmanuel Lévinas. (1986). "Dialogue with Emmanuel Lévinas." In *Face to Face with Lévinas*, edited by Richard A. Cohen. Albany: State University of New York Press.

King, H. R. (1950). "Aristotle's Theory of *Topos*." *Classical Quarterly* 44 (1 and 2): 77–96.

Kirby, Vicki. (1997). *Telling Flesh: The Substance of the Corporeal*. New York: Routledge.

Krell, David Farrell. (1992). *Daimon Life: Heidegger and Life-Philosophy*. Bloomington: Indiana University Press.

———. (1993). Introduction to *Martin Heidegger Basic Writings*, edited by David Farrell Krell. London: Routledge.

———. (1997). *Archeticture: Esctasies of Space, Time and the Human Body*. Albany: State University of New York Press.

Lacey, A. R. (1989). *Bergson*. London: Routledge.

Lawlor, Leonard. (2003). *The Challenge of Bergsonism*. London and New York: Continuum.

———. (2004). "What Immanence? What Transcendence? The Prioritization of Intuition over Language in Bergson." *British Journal of Phenomenology* 35 (1): 24–41.

——— (2006). *The Implications of Immanence: Toward a New Concept of Life*. New York: Fordham University Press.

Lear, Jonathan. (1988). *Aristotle: The Desire to Understand*. Cambridge: Cambridge University Press.

Liebniz, Gottfried Wilhelm. (1902). *Monadology*. In *Discourse on Metaphysics, Correspondence with Arnaud, Mondalogy*, translated by George Montgomery. La Salle, Ill.: Open Court.

Lévinas, Emmanuel. (1987). *Time and the Other*. Translated by Richard A. Cohen. Pittsburgh: Dusquesne University Press.

———. (1998). *Otherwise Than Being: or, Beyond Essence*. Translated by Alphonso Lingis. Pittsburgh: Dusquesne University Press.

———. (2000). *God, Death, and Time*. Translated by Bettina Bargo. Stanford: Stanford University Press.

Lingis, Alphonso. (1994a). *Abuses*. Berkeley: University of California Press.

———. (1994b). *The Community of Those Who Have Nothing in Common*. Bloomington: Indiana University Press.

———. (1994c). *Foreign Bodies*. New York: Routledge.

———. (1998). *The Imperative*. Bloomington: Indiana University Press.

———. (2000). *Dangerous Emotions*. Berkeley: University of California Press.

Lloyd, G. E. R. (1966). *Polarity and Analogy: Two Types of Argumentation in Early Greek Thought*. Cambridge: Cambridge University Press.

———. (1968). *Aristotle: The Growth and Structure of His Thought*. London: Cambridge University Press.

———. (1982). *Early Greek Science: Thales to Aristotle*. London: Chatto and Windus.

Lloyd, Genevieve. (1984). *The Man of Reason: "Male" and "Female" in Western Philosophy*. London: Methuen.

Lorraine, Tamsin. (1999). *Irigaray and Deleuze: Experiments in Visceral Philosophy*. Ithaca, N.Y.: Cornell University Press.

Lyotard, Jean François. (1991). "Matter and Time." In *The Inhuman: Reflections of Time*, translated by Geoffrey Bennington and Rachel Bowlby. Cambridge: Polity.

Mader, Mary Beth. (2003). "All Too Familiar: Luce Irigaray's Recent Thought on Sexuation and Generation." *Continental Philosophy Review* 36 (4): 367–90.

Martin, Alison. (2000). *Luce Irigaray and the Question of the Divine*. London: Maney.

Maritain, Jacques. (1968). *Bergsonian Philosophy and Thomism*. Translated by Mabelle L. Andison in collaboration with J. Gordon Andison. New York: Greenwood.

May, William. (1970). "The Reality of Matter in the Metaphysics of Bergson." *International Philosophical Quarterly* 10: 611–42.

Merleau-Ponty, Maurice. (1968). *The Visible and the Invisible*. Translated by Alphonso Lingis. Evanston, Ill.: Northwestern University Press.

———. (1988). *In Praise of Philosophy and Other Essays*. Translated by John Wild, J. Edie, and J. O'Neill. Evanston, Ill.: Northwestern University Press.

Moi, Toril. (1985). *Sexual/Textual Politics: Feminist Literary Theory*. London: Methuen.

Morison, Benjamin. (2002). *On Location: Aristotle's Concept of Place*. Oxford: Clarendon Press.

Mortensen, Ellen. (1994). "Woman's Untruth and *le féminin*: Reading Luce Irigaray with Nietzsche and Heidegger." In *Engaging with Irigaray: Feminist Philosophy and Modern European Thought*, edited by Carolyn Burke, Naomi Schor, and Margaret Whitford. New York: Columbia University Press.

———. (2002). *Touching Thought: Ontology and Sexual Difference*. Lanham, Md.: Lexington Books.

Mullarkey, John. (1999a). *Bergson and Philosophy*. Edinburgh: Edinburgh University Press.

———, ed. (1999b). *The New Bergson*. Manchester: Manchester University Press.

Nietzsche, Friedrich. (1954). *The Portable Nietzsche*. Edited by Walter Kauffman. Harmondsworth: Viking Penguin.

———. (1973). *Beyond Good and Evil*. Translated by R. J. Hollingdale. Harmondsworth: Penguin.

Olkowski, Dorothea. (1999). *Gilles Deleuze and the Ruin of Representation*. Berkeley: University of California Press.

———. (2000a). *Chiasm, the Interval of Sexual Difference between Irigaray and Merleau-Ponty*. In *Rereading Merleau-Ponty*, edited by Lawrence Hass and Dorothea Olkowski. New York: Humanity.

———. (2000b). "The End of Phenomenology: Bergson's Interval in Irigaray." *Hypatia* 15 (2): 73–91.

Organ, Troy Wilson. (1949). *An Index to Aristotle in English Translation*. Princeton: Princeton University Press.

Parisi, Luciana. (2004). *Abstract Sex: Philosophy, Bio-Technology, and the Mutations of Desire*. London: Continuum.

Perpich, Diane. (2003). "Subjectivity and Sexual Difference: New Figures of the Feminine in Irigaray and Cavarero." *Continental Philosophy Review* 36 (4): 391–413.

Peters, F. E. (1967). *Greek Philosophical Terms: A Historical Lexicon*. New York: University Press.

"Physis." (1996). *A Greek–English Lexicon*. 8th ed.

Plato. (1937). *Plato's Cosmology: The Timaeus of Plato: Translated, with a Running Commentary by Francis MacDonald Cornford*. Translated by Francis MacDonald Cornford. London: Kegan Paul.

———. (1961). Timaeus. Translated by Benjamin Jowett. In *The Collected Dialogues of Plato*, edited by Edith Hamilton and Huntington Cairns. New York: Bollingen Series.

———. (1970) *The Republic*. Translated by H. D. P. Lee. Harmondsworth: Penguin.

Prigogine, Ilya. (1997). *The End of Certainty*. New York: Free Press.

Rajchman, John. (1998). *Constructions*. Cambridge, Mass.: MIT.

———. (2000). *The Deleuze Connections*. Cambridge, Mass.: MIT.

Ronell, Avital. (1989). *The Telephone Book: Technology, Schizophrenia, Electric Speech*. Lincoln: University of Nebraska Press.

———. (1994). *Finitude's Score Essays for the End of the Millennium*. Lincoln: University of Nebraska Press.

———. (2002). *Stupidity*. Urbana and Chicago: University of Illinois Press.

———. (2005). *The Test Drive*. Urbana and Chicago: University of Illinois Press.

Ross, Sir David. (1964). *Aristotle*. London: Methuen.

Rouch, Hélène. (1987). "La placenta comme tiers." In "Le sexe linguistique," edited by Luce Irigaray. Special issue, *Languages* 85: 1–79.

Le Roy, Edouard. (1913). *A New Philosophy: Henri Bergson*. Translated by Vincent Benson. New York: Henry Holt.

Sambursky, S. (1956). *The Physical World of the Greeks*. Translated by Merton Dagut. London: Routledge and Kegan Paul.

———. (1962). *The Physical World of Late Antiquity*. London: Routledge and Kegan Paul.

Sanford, Stella. (2001). "Feminism against 'the Feminine.'" *Radical Philosophy* 105: 6–14.

Schor, Naomi. (1994). "The Essentialism Which Is Not One." In *Engaging with Irigaray: Feminist Philosophy and Modern European Thought*, edited by Carolyn Burke, Naomi Schor, and Margaret Whitford. New York: Columbia University Press.

Simondon, Gilbert. (1992). "The Genesis of the Individual." Translated by Mark Cohen and Sanford Kwinter. In *Incorporations*, edited by Jonathan Crary and Sanford Kwinter. Zone 6. New York: Zone.

Smith, Steven G. (2002). "The Mind–Matter Inversions: Bergson's Conception of Mental and Material Actuality." *The Southern Journal of Philosophy* 60 (2): 295–314.

Solmsen, Friedrich. (1960). *Aristotle's System of the Physical World*. Cornell Studies in Classical Philology 33. Ithaca, N.Y.: Cornell University Press.

Spivak, Gayatri Chakravorty. (1993). *Outside in the Teaching Machine*. New York and London: Routledge.

Stephen, Karin. (1922). *The Misuse of Mind: A Study of Bergson's Attack on Intellectualism*. London: Kegan Paul.

Stewart, Ian. (1990). *Does God Play Dice? The Mathematics of Chaos*. London: Penguin.

Stone, Alison. (2003). "Irigaray and Hölderlin on the Relation between Nature and Culture." *Continental Philosophy Review* 36 (4): 415–32.

Tuana, Nancy. (1989). "The Weaker Seed: The Sexist Bias of Reproductive Theory." In *Feminism and Science*, edited by Nancy Tuana. Bloomington: Indiana University Press.

Turnbull, Robert G. (1976). "'Physics' I: Sense Universals, Principles, Multiplicity, and Motion." In *Motion and Time Space and Matter*, edited by Peter K. Machamer and Robert G. Turnbull. Columbus: Ohio State University Press.

Urmson, J. O. (1990). *The Greek Philosophical Vocabulary*. London: Duckworth.

Vasseleu, Cathryn. (1998). *Textures of Light: Vision and Touch in Irigaray, Levinas, and Merleau-Ponty*. London: Routledge.

Wagner, Helmut R. (1983). *Alfred Schultz: An Intellectual Biography*. Chicago: Chicago University Press.

Ward, Julie, ed. (1996). *Feminism and Ancient Philosophy*. New York: Routledge.

Watson, Irene. (2002). "Aboriginal Laws and the Sovereignty of Terra Nullius." Borderlands 1(2) (2002). http://www.borderlands.net.au/vol1no2_(2002)/watson_laws.html.

Watson, Sean. (1998). "The New Bergsonism: Discipline, Subjectivity, Freedom." *Radical Philosophy* 92: 6–16.

Weinstein, Jami. (2004). Traces of the Beast: Becoming-Nietzsche, Becoming-Animal, and the Figure of the Trans-Human. In *A Nietzschean Bestiary: Becoming Animal beyond Docile and Brutal*, edited by Christa Davis Acampora and Ralph R. Acampora. Lanham, Md.: Rowman and Littlefield.

———. (2008). Introduction: II. In Deleuze and Gender, edited by Claire Colebrook and Jami Weinstein. Special issue of Deleuze Studies 2 (supplement): 20–33.

Weiss, Gail. (1995). "Ambiguity, Absurdity, and Reversibility: Responses to Indeterminacy." *Journal of the British Society for Phenomenology* 26 (1): 43–51.

———. (1999). *Body Images: Embodiment as Intercorporeality*. London: Routledge.

Whitford, Margaret. (1991). *Luce Irigaray: Philosophy in the Feminine*. London: Routledge.

Winkler, John J. (1990). *The Constraints of Desire: The Anthropology of Sex and Gender in Ancient Greece*. New York: Routledge.

Witt, Charlotte. (1999). "Form, Normativity and Gender in Aristotle: A Feminist Perspective." In *Feminist Interpretations of Aristotle*, edited by Cynthia A. Freeland. University Park: Pennsylvania State University.

Worms, Frederic. (1999). "Bergson's Matter and Memory." Translated by Pelagia Goulimari. In *The New Bergson*, edited by John Mullarkey. Manchester: Manchester University Press.

Young, Iris Marion. (1990). *Throwing Like A Girl and Other Essays in Feminist Philosophy and Social Theory*. Bloomington: Indiana University Press.

Zaner, Richard M. (1985). *The Problem of Embodiment: Some Contributions to a Phenomenonology of the Body*. The Hague: Nijhoff.

Ziarek, Ewa Plonowska. (2001). *An Ethics of Dissensus*. Stanford: Stanford University Press.

———. (2005). "Kristeva and Fanon: Revolutionary Violence and Ironic Articulation." In *Revolt, Affect, Collectivity: The Unstable Boundaries of Kristeva's Polis*, edited by Tina Chanter and Ewa Plonowska Ziarek. Albany: State University of New York Press.

INDEX